KALEIDOSCOPIC OMNISCIENCE

KALEIDOSCOPIC OMNISCIENCE

Will Alexander

Edited by Daniel Staniforth

© Will Alexander 2013

First published in Great Britain in 2013 by Skylight Press, 210 Brooklyn Road, Cheltenham, Glos GL51 8EA

All rights reserved. Except for the quotation of short passages for the purposes of criticism and review, no part of this publication may be reproduced, stored in a retrieval system or transmitted, in any form or by any means, electronic, mechanical, photocopying, recording or otherwise, without the prior consent of the copyright holder and publisher.

Will Alexander has asserted his right to be identified as the author of this work.

The First Edition of *Asia & Haiti* was published in 1995 by Sun & Moon Press for the New American Poetry Series 17, portions of which appeared in *Apex of the M* and *The Little Magazine*.

The First Edition of *The Stratospheric Canticles* was published in 1995 by Pantograph Press, portions of which appeared in *Apex of the M, First Intensity, Juxta, Mandorla, o blek* and *Sulfur*.

Designed and typeset by Rebsie Fairholm
Edited and formatted by Daniel Staniforth
Cover art and interior illustrations by Will Alexander

www.skylightpress.co.uk

Printed and bound in Great Britain by Lightning Source, Milton Keynes. Text set in Vulpa, a font by Schizotype. Titles set in Darjeeling, a font by FaceType.

British Library Cataloguing-in-Publication data:
A catalogue record for this book is available from the British Library.

ISBN 978-1-908011-49-7

For
JAYNE CORTEZ 1934-2012

she who spawned hurricanes in her speech

Contents

Introduction: Replete with Animation   11

Asia & Haiti

    Asia   17
    Haiti   65

The Stratospheric Canticles

    The Mime Tornado   115
    The Psychotropic Squalls   116
    The Mesmeric Remora   118
    Song in Barbarous Fumerole of the Japanese Crested Ibis   121
    Against the Temperature of Time & Corrosion   128
    Apprenticeship   131
    Explosive Decibel Journeys   134
    The Stratospheric Canticles   138

Impulse & Nothingness

    Impulse & Nothingness   179
    Utopian Parallel Intensity   181
    Rays from the Biographic X-ray Chalice   183
    The Recidivous Concubine of Dimness   184
    Entropy as the Bone Queen   187
    The Monsoon Queen of the Soul   189
    Call to My Flaming Starfish Shakti   190
    Oblique Sensorial Savagery   192
    Subtractive Venery   194
    Candle from the Black Widow's Love Cake   197
    To My Savage Muscatel Lady   199

Wavering Rumination on Ontology	202
Remorse & Infinity	203
The Vaporous Cortical Field	204
Augury	206
Dauntless Cimmerian Farming	207
Bewitchment from the Radium Furnace	207
Between History & Omniscience	209
The Final Poltergeist of Pompeii	214
Grasp at an Unknown Existence	217
An Odd Neuteria	218
Hellenistic Camouflage	218
The Rising Eye	219
Volatility	219
Alchemic Moray's Reversal	220
Loss from Malediction & Exile	220
Breaking Through Linguistic Reason	222
Toward the Endless Vertex Summit	224
Astrobiology	225
Desertion & Concealment	226
Bioluminal Self-Seeing	233
Clairvoyant Hummingbird's Braille	235
Sumatran Mirror World	236
Within the Oracular Seahorse Mirror	237
The Cryptographic Ocelot	241
The Water Dog	245
A National Day in Bangladesh	249
Anti Euro-Psychosis	252
Modernity	254
Bridge as Poisonous Anti-Harvest	255
Albania & the Death of Enver Hoxha	257
Glossary	263
Editor's Postscript	273

List of illustrations

The Monsoon & its Metrics	119
Angelic Equilibrium	127
The Subconscious Eye	139
Volcano of Birds	157
In the Abstract Silurian Sea	175

Introduction

"...The poet shocks those around him. He speaks openly of what authority has deemed as unspeakable..."
— Bob Kaufman

I swim in the void
In the blaze of the sun I tremble
I quiver among the shadows
And I float on the mists
— Vincente Alexiandre

Replete with Animation

As poet I've been blessed with the instinct for hearing. I've always been filled with herds of sound from the moment I gained my first aural realization. Summed in five words: the electrical instinct for language. This instinct has provided me with self-possessive industry, allowing me to continuously rise into an elevated aural field. And by industry I mean continuous tilling of the mind, so that over time verbal crops are unleashed. To paraphrase Rimbaud, I is another. Respiration on this plane takes place by means of alchemic treason. Assumption by means of the old mechanical methods need be mentally abducted and slain. Without such action mechanical method becomes a carking fuel which entangles the alchemic. Thus, the ear becomes foiled through effort at quotidian confirmation. The latter leading to safety through domestic adjustment. Aversion then condenses as barrier against uncertainty. Thus, failure ensues as regards to inscribing an alien encryption with one's thinking.

Through praxis, I've come to understand that a poet remains at another level than a journalist, the latter always racing to illumine the particulars from pre-received consciousness. Contrary to this, the poet is always striking out across the inferno of the self, taking chances by means of self-experiment. It is an inner wandering which allows one to speak without the aid of second thinking. For instance, linking in one breath the incommensurate duality of Flanders and the Congo, thereby weaving an incandescent mural of the world. Which means, all sources of contact are germane to poetic speech. And one need not be expert on grain farming, or Egyptian mystical practice, but one needs an accurate feel for the core principle of the subject at hand. It is like tasting the poetic carbon which saturates the details. And it is from this depth that the taste and burning of words transpires. In a word, foment, which transmutes the aural mind by means of an invisible acrobatics. A non-measurable energy, if you will, which is incapable of being stymied by the verbal field which sires the provincial domain, of say, sibling rivalry, or the perpetual quest for prestige.

Simply put, the interior state. This being the zone where aural volcanoes begin blooming. For instance, a spark which ignites as the flooded luminosity of an ampersand, rushing into the mind with unbidden focus. This being the power which appears from untamed regions, called by some, the raw, the unintentional, by others, the bleak, the unadorned, the unsettled. Myself, I call it unstudied purity.

For me, this is what I understand to be fertility of background, the background most suitable for engaging the world of invaluable texts. Study then becomes refinement of one's inner hearing, so much so, that the kinetics of consciousness begins brewing unsought lingual possibilities.

This was the state from which *Kaleidoscopic Omniscience* arose. As is my natural wont, I've always been entranced by the contagion of the kaleidoscopic. During the nascent years of the last decade of the previous century the poetic began to well in me to an extraordinary degree. It was during this reign of inspiration that I wrote *Asia & Haiti*, *The Stratospheric Canticles*, and *Impulse and Nothingness* as well as my novel *Sunrise In Armageddon*.

The three books of poems form an organic constellation. Their range extends from the flora and fauna of Tibet, to new world politics and culture in Haiti, doubling back to Italy and ideology under Hoxha in Albania, combined with my interest in the mystery of the cosmos. Intertwined with these locales there is engagement with areas such as ecology, and world painting, as well as with the psychosis of dictatorship.

Of the three volumes, *Asia & Haiti* has had the most public impact. Beautifully published by Douglas Messerli and Sun and Moon Press in 1995, it has remained an enduring document since the time of its first appearance. Yet it comes a time for engagement with new readership, and I feel now is a propitious time to re-ignite it into the world. *The Stratospheric Canticles* published in the same

Introduction

year has engaged in a less extrinsic life, yet has always engaged in organic respiration with *Asia & Haiti*. It was published through the good offices of Ivan Arguelles and Andrew Joron at Pantograph Press. It originally included my cover drawing aptly entitled *The Stratospheric Canticles*. I also illustrated its interior staging with pencil drawings, and the whole was superbly designed by Robert Frazier. As for *Impulse & Nothingness*, it has remained the invisible member of the trilogy. Announced over the years as forthcoming it has never appeared in collected form. True, many of its poems appeared in publications such as *Sulfur* and *Exquisite Corpse*, yet it has remained this summoning poltergeist just out of reach. There was always the genuine desire by Green Integer to publish the volume, but delay has begat delay, so the volume has been compelled to its destiny through absence.

Now that the situation has cleared, all three volumes can now appear as one. *Kaleidoscopic Omniscience* encompasses all the tendencies of the volumes in a unified field. They can now respire as the spectra of one Sun. In closing, I want to thank Daniel Staniforth and Skylight Press for making this union replete, and newly active in the world.

WILL ALEXANDER

Āsia & Haiti

For SARA NOKOMIS WEIR
You who eternally hover in magnetic aequiliritus

Asia

> ... through reasonings such as the
> present birth's becoming a past
> birth when the future birth becomes
> the present birth, one identifies
> that past, present, and future
> births are mutually dependent and
> thus do not exist inherently.
> — JEFFREY HOPKINS
> *Meditation all Emptiness*

> You who are not imprisoned in the
> flesh, who know at what point in
> its carnal trajectory, its senseless
> comings and goings, the soul
> finds the absolute verb, the new
> word, the inner land ...
> — ANTONIN ARTAUD
> *Letter To The Buddhist Schools*

The voice in this poem is a collective voice of rebellious Buddhist monks who hover in invisibility, vertically exiled, in an impalpable spheroid, virescently tinged, subtly flecked with scarlet, conducting astral warfare against the Chinese invasion and occupation of Tibet. Their originating zone, "the great Sera Monastery, a focal point of anti-Chinese feeling four miles" outside "of Lhasa." — W.A.

"Let us recall the illusion:
the thousands murdered
the texts exploded
the sun become
a mechanical sub rosa

we
the once green wings of a magical Tibet
accused by the Maoists
by the exterior flames of ideology & assault

the insults
the curses
the fierce & poisonous scaling ores
endured
buried by general anthrax & demon

yet we've emerged
with our murmurs
with our saffron bleeding above the 12 illusive zones of the zodiac
with our bleak & tested fatigue
able to concentrate our blindings
our spectral condensation
to roaming steam
to tragic pints of venom

our fate ensnared
by Chinese materia
by dyslexic simian diversion

by we
of seeming maximal debility
the spiders swarming in our mantras
throughout this canticle of purges

we
exiled
in this green electrical penumbra
looking down
on this heinous
monochromatic Pentecost
on Marxist grafting
by furnace & foreclosure
pulled from our shrouded mantric chambers
to do wonders for the scions
for the misanthropic whaling dolls
stunted in their core by brutality

these drab & scaly Marxists
plotted by erasure

by procedure by burden
by churlish transposition of the conflagrant spirit sun

this has been our lot in exile
inside this magic virescent penumbra
spinning our prayer wheels
above our leaking opium explodents
above our fulgurant supernal yeasts

we
spawned from the ethers
by coupled monkey & demon *
by incandescent boiling rods

so be it
in this primeval penumbra
in this heightened verdigris scarlet
in this incisive analogical omniscience
it is we
who break the bells wide open
it is we
who signal the dead in their post-mortem frenzy
with a turbulent flame of Yaks
with dense in-vital stuffing lynxes
with mixture by forboding & conundrum

for us
this is path by treacherous lightning analogy
by magic & blowing grass at the snow line

for us
the true interior Tibet
of dark & irreversible surcease
tearing down the dialectical habitat
with structures
from our darkened Bon endowment *
kaleidoscopic with vermin
with spells
with fabulous eradications & wildness

so we are ensconsed
concentrated
with the non-rectangular
with savagery

we aspire to Nirvana
to be left unsullied
like vertical plumes
from a yurt on fire with potassics
we do not live in Rotational scarlet
to dwell on Mesozoic geology
or speak of arguments & counter-arguments
concerning instinctive erasure & existence

so when we speak of the 'west-east' direction of the 'Pamirs'
or the 'Taurus Mountains along the southern edge of Turkey'
or the ashen 'edge of the Iranian Plateau'
it is the 'ligature of our throats
of our prognostic blazes

we whose empiric is vapour
whose high cylindrical interior
burns throughout a rudimentary balance
throughout a transparent hemlock

we in this floating Boschian domain
squalid
hierarchical
frenzied

recall
the leprous empirics
of the Chinese invasion

disheartened by brigades
the Dalai Lama recalls
'three men in grey suits ...
who looked extremely drab
Communists

with their bland dehumanized debasement
with their fired material anger
with their vicious legerdemains against Lhasa
against our wild & alien Sino burning
against our scrolls
against the singing of our daughters in judgement

therefore our flaming
our rooted sheafs
our Nāgārjunian strangeness *
then the revolts
then the musics from our dungeons of blood

'The Chinese demanded
that' we supply their troops with food
& according to the 'Minister'
'Tsepon Shakabpa' *
pushed our people
to the 'verge of famine'

so we 'spat at them'
'sang rude songs about them'
hit them with 'knots' 'tied' in our prayer 'shawls'

we
from the Sera enclave *
we
the first the cycle of resistance
joined the warlike Khambas *
so that 'bridges' were 'destroyed'
'columns' 'attacked'
our actions in keeping with Nāgārjuna's relativity
with his asp like sniping
at chains of total domination

for we are a people who cease to flinch at panic
we who feast on 'tsamba' *
on tea with rancid butter
our imported barley 'compressed into bricks'

our exports of gold dust & borax
for we breathe the fumes of heaven
from our high plateau of camels
from our astral antelopes & leopards
we soar
with convergent dilation
with the wizardry & stamina of sealing
we who hail
from 'Srongtsan Gompa' *
first Tibetan king
who brought the first instructive allonyms

then we rose
to high status amongst the Mongols
we who flourished
at the court at Karakorum *
then the reforms of Tsong-khapa *
then the title of Dalai Lama as conferred by Altun Khan *

therefore
whatever we owed to China
'we owed to the vanished dynasty'
our ancient Chinese relations
a furnace of old diaries
now the Communists
forgers
liars
the 17 point Agreement *
falsified as coding
not the true insistence of our destiny
nor the karma of our fiery backdrop

we've suffered retreats
by negative copulation
by copulation by insincerity
road building labour
murderous dictation by Marx

we remember our 'God-King Lama'
'Clutching a rifle'
'dressed as a Khamba guerrilla'
escaping

to the 'rebel' interior 'of Loka' *
with 'Rinchen Dolma Taring' *
who prayed to her '*karma* deity'
for the bodies left behind

'the ferocious hand to hand fighting'
the thousands left bleeding
against fulminate walls & markings

we
with the power of Padma Sambhava *
who subjected local demons
to the power of the faithful
his spirit revived
above ignited 'peaks' of honour
above magical realms of transparency
this is our grandeur
the true enkindled species of our name

the intense empirical emptiness
floating inside our heated wafting sphere
in this mental omniscience
in the wake of this Chinese Imperial seismology
where our glass was broken
our angels dishonoured
a tragic waking dread
& each symbol of eternity
crushed & scattered
inside a black & winding eclipse maze

an auricular mumbling
a grating against veins

now
we take into account the *topos* of the hypocrites
the British
who treated us like pyres
like maggots to be burned
we who aspire
to the asperated death
to imperishable circulation

therefore
we give to the Dalai Lama
our thigh bone intoning
our mesmerizing drafts
our moral invictas

in this high insistence of writhing
we
of pre-existent living enigmas
of secretive bell groups & readings

we
who have thrived
on less visible statics
on our sullen & cloudless phoneme confluence
we who have founded the impermissable
the deathless floating through emotional locales
who have practiced degrees of shattering & confinement

of starvation & loss by conditional maiming
we who have formed
exquisite bodily resistance
having merged with the fires of negated causal pauses
inside
of buried auroras
of selective dissonance treaties

therefore
our dense prohibitive rootings
our pointless flailing scapels

our heaving eclipse ruins
hewing the void
with our isolated weathers
we
of weightless jonquil species
as in an in-judicious cometary fable
as in a star with useless stratagems & burnings
which explodes from incessance & negation of labour
thus we ascend
to particles of Nirvana
the first extinguished beings to vibrate

'Vasubandhu' *
'Dignāga' *
'Dharmakīrti' *
a lineage of savants
founders of disputations & draftings
so as
to eradicate lizards

to bundle sensate forces into dunes which scatter
into elemental faeces
into smokeless illusives

the rubric
the deadened clandestine walls
all fictive
all hallucinatory sub-plots of atoms

& we are diversified
only as to games
as to dark & wayward parabolas which stricken
which flare up & strengthen the waking mood of desolation

these
the arguments of our goal
as we leap towards anti-existence

to transcend the path
by vertical cyclone lavas
to take from our fingers
the stitches of ravens
the crude & particular music of despair
yes
the infortuitous force of oppositional beheading

therefore
the tumultuous
the less than living spasmodic anathema
dissolved

& reborn
& spinning as post-Chaldean plottings
for we
from the bonfire of discipline
of stunning in-facilitas rewards
we who have thrown shards from the mangers of oblivion
into loosely splintered enclaves
precisely at the point
of a winding aggregate mono-dimension
a flattened haze of wafting particle structure
where even forbearers sink
into the motion of illusion

those 'ferocious barbarian shepherds'
who sacrificed
'sheep'
& 'dogs'
& 'monkeys'
who communed with 'knotted cords'
with 'pieces of wood'
who from our common simian father
came the love of piety & higher somnambulance & good
& from our she-devil mother
sprang the 'roughness'
'cruelty'
'ferocity'

& deceit
so the spores of jealousy
the ink of locusts
the extremes of wolves
all combined in shadow
from which we rise
singing with extinguished groans
with old magnetic jute & ringing
we who refuse to dissolve into error
into burning or shredded rums which implode

we
with fanatic obedience
to the levels which melt coetaneous existence
to soporific perfection
to mime by ravaged volcano & cunning

the Chinese terror
like the 'Euleuth Tartars' storming 'from Jungaria' *
are burdens we oppose
engendered by strife
by storm & dissolution
by weakened trespasser's cinders

a bared & ceaseless emptiness
of traceless caliginous phosphors
through which we float throughout our darkened Bon beginnings
averting the fires of old declared inversions
we invent the exploded coffin
the rising of cups in the air through volcanoes
it is we
throughout the incandescent living eras

weaving salt from seeming oracular mirages
from bound tubercular freezings
found
in the unbuttered tea brick
in the 'Kingku Dut'ang' drank by 'Lamas' & the 'wealthy' *
in the 'Gewa Dut'ang' drank by the 'better classes'

in the 'Chensi' & the 'Kingku Dhuni' 'ripe' & of 'good colour'
in the 'Shāchin Dhuni' the highest popularity
in the 'Shalu' & the 'Chuba' the imbibed of the 'poorer classes''
in the flavour of the 'Pet'ang' drank for its positive monarchical brilliance
then
the 'Gyeba' at the lowest
with the poorest claim to addition by butter

then
our Tibetan importations
of 'silks' & 'carpets' from 'China'
of 'leather' & 'horses' from 'Mongolia'
of 'indigo' & 'brasswork' from 'Nepal'
of 'saffron' & 'dried fruits' from 'Ladak'
of various 'articles from India'

then
from our homeland the 'obvious Game'
from the 'Chumbi Valley' *
the 'Tragopan'
in the 'pine' & 'rhododendron woods'
the 'blood pheasant' strutting amidst lichen 'green rocks'
'on the upper hills'

'musk-deer'
above the air of the trees
'herds of blue sheep'
then the 'Brown-shouldered Tiger-cat'
the 'Jackals'
the 'Martens'

if we speak as mystic cannibals
or darkened scorpion dwellers from on high
it is because
we know existence to be nameless
to burn in flameless quaternary battles
fuelled by opacity
by the thought of great hunger & schism

floating
'along the sacred circular road'
'past straggling files' of human pylon & kindling
'passing gardens' & 'orchards' & 'shaggy stretches of woodland'
we can't condemn our powers
or react with nervous blistering
as to our strange & unresolved galvanic catoptrics
therefore a rendezvous
a handicapped expression in the mind

we no longer act
with brazen optical breads
or with 'the red-capped Sarus crane'
always painted in Japan with beguilement

as if we relished
unembarkable cancellation
in each solemn fact of our electrical personae
as if we were rain
or drifting 'Cobalt Warblers'
summoned to withdrawal by inscrutable contradiction
giving the void an optics
a magical translation of prairies
throughout a flaming set of principles
from a partial bank
from a mistrusted foci

therefore
bramble as logos
surname as pontificate

we
who plunge
through inherent existence
who surmount as beast
restrictive gallstone as landscape
or asps who burn with thriving spittle

it is we who send up smoke through the archives
it is we who live in wakeless daylight threadings
so as to throttle the tincture of thankless monsters
so as to reach with our brooding the very chronicles of error

it is we who seek divestiture
who seek loss by staining & the rubric of models

it is we
who break the lamp of lidless miming covers
who assault each vaporous schism & the sunlight as whole
yes
we interrogate murmurs
& all the hidden cholera of bone ferns
of cyclopic eels & demons
flickering with harassment

it is we who summon
the analytical
the briberies
the strange misogynist's pincers

each stake in our mental refinement
reveals the deeper aurum in our destiny
the deeper proof of our release
as if anointed
with a poisonous virgin's withdrawal

so it is
that we specify an ink
as a diadem that summons its refulgence from splendour
as a substance voided & renounced by sensation

this is the moment
the arcanum as monument
the fervour
the chanting
the sudden appearance as flaw

we have failed at social daring
& come to this wafting
whose pinnacle is a vial
exploded by nerves
by salvos of wild in-palatial explosives

this is our odyssey
our plight
& our honour
to re-kindle absence
without greenish biopsies or strife

thus
you see the law
the risings
in each of our substanceless blazings & distance

thus
we animate logistics
as liberation from dread
from pessimistics
from contradiction
giving rise to many dawns in abysses

thus we forestall old ironies & judgements
& forge new atoms with ferocious light from doubled solar ores
this is the anti-cacophonous
the harmony against barrier by dysfunction

therefore it is
that we give forth bells
& henceforth harmony from bells

we
the old fiery Lamas from the ocean
from the great green thrones of infinity

we
the cataclysmic

the hunchbacked harmonia in fragments
as though we could forage for *selvas* or ponies
through a tense immigration of storms & chastisements

here we are linked
to skilled & unreasoning petrifaction as dice
as pylons of thirst
as haunted frankincense & chasms
devoid of atomics
of levitational timings
to invoke subterfuge
kinesis
creating arrested flanks in the moon & its bastions

in this untamed refuge
we are argument for the object as fecund subtractive
as folly by 'inherent existence'

summoned from high arroyos & arches
our eyes flow with the fervour of retreating neutrinos
of buried divinings
of suspensions in orbit

it is we who burn as a watch clock
as lifeless angel-worm annealments
brought to deeper post-mortem galvanics
to a fever which strengthens against opaque & landless
increments & patterns

we who sought our living in ceaselessness
in explosive argon deliverance
as if our stomas were mirrored in smoking phosphorous caves
as benign abnegation
as sigils by protective armasa invasion *

so the skull is useless
as sundered omnivorous cathedral
as ironic surge of transmuted voltage

so by hewing explosive harbours from mountains
we take rain fall at Yamdok Lake *
at Sivok *
at Tarkhola *

we speak of iodine by flying
by faultless drinking gorge & chimeras

then the snow from the upper skyline
the high Saturnian moon over Lhasa
as if we were lighted by a wilfully bleeding candle of oxide
or a sinking pervasive aurora by invasion
therefore
a probity by ethers

by prolifically worked odoriferous acres

we of lucidity & signals
ceasing to cling to our province
to those annihilated settings
governed by shadowed barley & granite
therefore
each impartial glance
each critical tree
as storm before advancement

therefore
it is we who plunged into summary as flame
into speaking as drift
as blank heretical conclusives
with an endless stare
of variety as repulsion
we speak
as bleached gregarious semaphores
as denied umbilical clarities
with the seismic zeal of darkened speculation

we are not a Devendrabuddhi *
concerned with literal simplicities

but as the Cashmere school or the followers of Prajnākara Gupta *
like a fall of great weight through the flames of Dharmakīrti
none of whose concerns bespeak a tortured allegation
nor thought as focus through stinging linear marrow
it is the focal contrast
not as a desperate singular personality

but as depth
as a transverse
as expulsion through memory

as to wind pollination
as to lateral angiosperm
we are quiescent
magnetized back to emptiness
hypnotically ascribed to the deepest burning lessons of thought

for us
the inference & remarks in the depths of Dharmakīrti
of the Buddha's 'Cosmical Body'
'in its twofold aspect'
of 'Absolute Existence'
& 'Absolute' as 'Knowledge'

we
the focused spells of 'Buddhist Logic'
we
the Tibetan
of Sa-skya-pandita *
of Rendapa-Zhonnu-lodoi *
beings we hold in 'high esteem'
beings who float in the amplitudes
into mimed forensic patterns
& soar
like opalescent fish
or blistered philosophical fowl pairing in the branches
like weightless mental sparring at a threshold of diamonds
like a glancing sun & its life between sparks

thus
the subsumed & radical midnight of atoms
the blanks
the high zodiacal wars
transcended
& we
green with Buddhist synonyms of proof
of absence at the peak of rotational glistening
of voided stories of gold
which feast upon blood sport
therefore
to inflame our mirrors as formless ingestion
takes on the bold relief of gravitational deception
ferociously lit
beneath the falling of the Pleiades
forcing our dictation
into old
warped
Brahmanical dharmas
of the Nyāya school *
with its maimed approach to ubiquitous externals
'Time'
'Space'
'The Cosmical Ether'
as posited externalities
as ferocious figments
fused with separate 'Inherence'
their motions incised with punishing charisma
empowered by random manacles
by apparitions scorched in their separated boundaries

we see
the personal carved
by scathing multiple divisions
each body split off & lettered with burins
with wayward perceptual sclerosis
searching in its stupor
for a nunnery of plankton
for a process to seal its insights with coldness

with partial turpentine mixed with seeming clarified mascara
it seeks in itself to stay broken
to keep itself erected by feelings superfluous with poison
each
with marred coronal blizzards
stunned inside their turquoise hamlets
eking to solve mortality riddles
the personal
with its flameless singularity
with motifs & other blindings of the a-clairvoyant 'Nihilists'
of darkened stammering crystal
before the one illusive judge across atomic infinity

life as such fatal exposure
is the serpent's penetration of despair
this being the judgement of the one single life
of the cold odoriferous portion
of the stagnant & unrelished projection

for instance
replacing flame with a scolding suspicion
with a wick of unblemished authority
advancing towards a reasoned model

as though its torment had ceased to exist
because
we've come to identify
substance as substanceless body
the accords
the breeches
the moments
the writhings
because
emptiness as essence
glow as non-dividing

the inklings
the veins between chasms

to know each paradox in its twilight
in its substanceless bleeding
in its motionless biding

therefore
thinking by cyclonic paroxysm
by methods which cease
their harmful & derailed oblivions

there are days
when the subject entrances a burden
& collapses in shadow
like bone against glass

these are the steps which we plough
chipping inch by inch
the squalid mangrove soil
the distance induced by asomatous solar magenta

hypnology
then the dream between two partings
between sun fed lightnings
& the animals in the sun

so against their rubicon
against their lucid & culminating odour
there is the leaking wind
the verdurous infusion
the chemical divided
by a throne over spiders

so
to speak of a plaintive ambit
or a ruined & intensified colossus
we must remember that we are soaked
in simple velocious conundrum
suspended & prowling
without the raging heat
for a harp or a furnace

a-symmetrical with powers
our lives advance
like a coruscating mask
in uneven darkness

so
as a seamless hourly menace
as continuous fleece across the signs of creation
we fire our intestinal raindrops
like in-fortuitous plagues
when burdened with inherence
when seen as posited cure
clinging with extinction

inherence
no more than a vile & stammering brilliance
a rendered particle
an in-susurrant tree

as if we could summon wild imaginal algaes
or a bailiff leaning on a doctrine of rays
so as to plough the fields
with chipped & flaming cometary rounds

then we could proceed to pursue concomitant procedures
with continuous facts
with smoking mirages

instead we summon unalterable co-tangents
like fresh water poured into identical viridity
as fiery star
as empty sun
that glows as fire
inside its anti-intention

therefore
in-seasonal pyroclastic
winding its way as motionless dispersion
through merging paradox ridiculed

with clarified transparency
opening its splendour
to unpredictable dictation
to formless deluge
to burning veneer

because
it is to take from its conduct
ceaseless degrees
ontological conclusives
fixed & rigid laryngeals which burden
which deftly describe
in small & toneless moisture which deafens

for us
there are the three rotating persons
of alien bodily glare
then its rising from old transfixture
then its thirst which blankly moves
beyond the cycle of all inherence

then the being emerges
into a thirstless non-condition
into emptiness as living circular evanescence

a vermiculate chiaroscuro
a windless 'transmission' of 'potencies'
not ghastly
or threatening with encroachment
but the boundless flank of solemn aggregates unwinding
the blood explosively cleaned
in the smokeless dearth of rudimentary plasma
then
charisma as person
as transfixed relativity
across extruded glacial sands
to investigate its model
its savagely kindled turning glints
like the odyssey of a million gradual suns arising

fantastical with enigma
with mysterious kinds of pillage
empiric with detonation
with distilled Olympian magnetics

the person being
a burning wick on a throne
an impeccable scar
glowing with balance
blown
to the deeper life of hearing
to the next rising sun of oviparous solar intangibles

& each mountain of pressure
each peal, of existence
like a transparent shard
like ruthless monumental ruin

become
a wild & analogous blemish
a resurrected captive
scarred by reasoning inherence
by small & despicable motives
which captivate the ions
in structured leonine affairs

nothing more
than the tragically enchained realms
of indecisive seismographies
but at a higher introspection
the whirling mind
as emptied mirror & its sundogs
like a penetrant ray
with miraculous training eye
peering through conceptions
with an unsevered spell
with in-canonical telepathy
nomadic as a plethora
bloodless with blizzards

as blank & unassailable conveyance
of ethers across the void

to make us myrmecophagous
or static with imbibing
would create for the viewer
eclectic presidios
unscalable testing points
unmeasurable dawning grounds

we could then no more move
as in a strange vitrescence with locusts
or with wrathful Myrmidons
or Jackals

so we of expressed volcanoes
of explosive Orphic range
concur with a seepage in calcareous asylum
emptied of caloricity
as a blank tasteless powder
a cathartic
an anti-calvaria
an exploded camarilla

we
without copper
gold
or iron
with starless letters in our fingers
drifting
with obliquely balanced ctenophores

or more specific
a voracious fire of halidoms
of encrypted hallucinosis
of translucent sycophants

these latter we abjure
we cancel in their literal tenor

only seeking from their realms
the power of the sigil

therefore
the secrecy brewing
the shadows unlettered
in the doves of various angles

we
the diaphanous
we
the cerulean mime cacophony
divested
from bigoted struggles & syntax
above pestiferous claims
repetitious with the dice of arrogance
a singing pedagogical somnifics
casting in rich collaborator's anthems
a motionless shark
a paradoxical oasis

the subtractive
the emptied
the barren

so we ask
what is the fate of inherence?
what are its principles?
its lodges?
its perpetual rigidity & lack of unfoldment?

it ceases to live in the motion of it absence
as to its raffish secondary fate
as to its post-mortem glaring
there no longer reigns a sovereign mortal aesthetics
a surface
an in-pierceable boundary
clamouring for a scope of allegorical confinement

one cannot protect the 'Inherent'
& its philosophy of obdurate heliotropes
its distillation to despicable hellgrammites
can never dispel the fiendish idea
of its motionless
unsubsiding haemochrome

& what of ironic cyclical inherence?
what of its shackles?
its blockage?
its further arising?

what concerns the play of its parts?
the logic of its roundelays?

its figments?
its churnings?
across a separated troposphere?

& so it is seen
as intensified self-birthing?
as dense sectarian delusion?
as splintered in a flawless axial field?

or is it sensate mass congealed within catharsis?

we who float
in high auricular suspension
bereft of moats
of dense rectangular germinations
as leprosy turned round
within a scarlet insomnia

thus
the raving claim for in-seminal dramatics
for wry & ventriloquized abutments which torture
merely the bounded
the parenthetical
the extruded rung
the force fed personality

for us
the particular stands as a carious iguana
as self-sufficient penance
subject to rot
to a cycle of glandular malfeasance
each life construed
as doomed & curious chapter
each summons to living plagiarized by opaqueness
a plight entangled in mirthless reification

the galling terms of a cauterized anatomy
of a contrived & blistered readiness to burn

these are the methods of transmogrified depression
ruthlessly kindled
through threat by blinking Stygian moons

the limbs
without action
stunned into fevers
into pre-directed forces
which dazzle without portent

the point being
a Yak in motion
a series of exterior glossaries condensed
in strange botanical causeways
from 'Yamdok Lake'
across the 'Kamba Pass' *
with startling inherence
with tinctures of apparent perception
the Yak
bionomic with chimera
from 'the valley of the Tsangpo' *
up the peaks of the 'Lord' & 'The White-Horned Lady' *
disappears through vertical columns
as a strange alchemical soldier of burden
a darkly enveloped mystagogue
now a beautiful peculiar treatise on absence

as if one were staring
at the void of the 'Garhwal Himalayas' *
at the ciphered visage of the 'Changt'ang plateau' *
with its sheep & great stags

one then understands
the paramount of the baseless
the shadowy
the imponderable

to wash with water the smoke from green fingers
from the garrulous compacting
of snails in a figure

one then scatters
the clinging somnifics
the spells
the reasons for the claims
of old Calliope & vertigo

the neuralgia
the lure
for the crazed mentalities of Titans

then
the great parallel a-rhythmias
the phobias
the mange
the intransigence

so it is
that our microbes burn
with our faces suspended
above a dark illuminant gorge

& we
not with the eye
but with the onerous consummation of the cells
exhibit faith in passionate sobriety
in lakeless coloratura

not the wild intensive kindlings
nor the droughts
nor the barren exposure to mechanics
but dioramas
celestial dioramas
glistening into pyres that rise into nocturnal splittings
into pantheons that float
into a tottering synopsis

not linear deepening
but emptiness
not conquest
but the void & the absence which binds it

therefore
the migrations
across green illuminant brilliance
against rhymed & galloping quadrupeds
against enriched coronal lapses
then again the void
& the paradox which binds its flames in absence

not
as atomic contingency
but throughout the momentary powers
& the roaming
& the fire that inform them
as the specifically haunted account
& the field of primal disconnection
between selves & anti-selves
rising into fusion
by sonority
by calm & stabilized abiding
by contained & dialectical watch works of irony
we have come to this condition
to this level
which the suns transfix
allowing us flight
beyond a cold & microbial brokenness

we exist in this sphere
as stated minimal collusion
of drafts
blowing & swirling in a sea beyond moons
in a high & circuitous equity
in this
we resemble an echo of blizzards
like a storm of rays
fallen from stars
we being the liminal
the asymptotic gradient

between the ghost of the rays & the stars
we being
the upper intention of darkness
the displaced & floating cyclical doors
through which we merge
with a curious voltage of turquoise
with a great dissemination of dust
like a curious stationary grandeur
formed from cageless dromedary angels
balanced in lightning
with densely streaked shapes & alembics

no
we are not a displaced semantics
or deforestation
or the drainage of glass
but the electrics of water
brought to the pinnacle of motionless snowfall ranges

for instance
the shape inside a blistered platinum stupa
would only magnetize a boiling Occident
would only petrify its waters
into probing for concreteness
so as to give
each particular stupa a date
a hounding clawed with supercilious navamsas *

with gliding zones increased throughout the pentads
so therefore
there is frenzy for result
for the lawless integer combined amidst bodies

as flawed astrology & counting
the planets' motions in slivered beast canals
in Brownian specificity
of messages planned with mathematical combining
the countings
the abstracts
the failures

the lost & motionless phase of war
of susurrant cranial pillage
of dark anathema as dove

yes
the findings
the astrological vapours
the anthropomorphic screens
the mechanically counted angels in order

here again
body as inherence
as the factual realm of post-mortem binding

the Venusian
the hissing
the surreptitious concubines
the serpents
the strange malevolence of connivance

therefore
destiny as Bardo
as mantra in tentative opprobrium

& the opprobrium of nightmare
as duality in post-mortem being

of monsters that flow from prior calendrical pondering
from cretonous flashings of former contrivance
is broken by holding centred
& breaking through each corrupted staggering signal
then the central catharsis unfolds
like synclinal & precipitous phosphors
through thronged & canonized dispersals
into a rudimentary plasma of bliss

a substance brought to sudden pitches
by a referent in the mind
by diagrams balanced by sudden nomadic angles
therefore
the body dispersed through mirrors
flowing as a spectrum
through exploded mental prolixities
then fixation exchanged for wild anaemias of delving
for deep & variant burnings of the soul
the tense & in-navigable training variations
the seeming systemic rot
the sudden oracular modelling as vision

& we ask ourselves
what is death?
what is the force of its blighted cyclical incisions?

so to rise above broken chances & treaties
to disallow identity by fearsome loss & confusion

we speak of combat as given
of broken flags in eclipsing dictations

as if monuments revealed an essence
or a *raison d'être* for forthright oblivion

our concrete nitrogen as moisture
our masses of granite as 'pure quartz' & 'felspar'
not as antiphony
or as canorous folly

but as 'faith'
'aspiration'
'exertion'
'pliancy'

we absolved
of unstable anathema
of voices that whisper under covered ponds of crystal
therefore
we exist as intensity
as blank communal bursts
as climax beyond all rancorous blessing

each glance
each burst
each target & bickering
pulled above cadaverous substrata

what of its kinship?
its dire & despicable flailing oscillations?
its illusive crests?
its blackened hydrangeas?

it appears & disappears
it cataclysmically wanders & blends without boundary
so the bodily being dissolves
& we
as conscious devastating ghosts
understand a rectangular intuitive evanescence
the stately omega of flashing indigent's doors
we who have known 'the high surgery' of surcease
the massive loss of concentrated pivots

it is we with the force
with the power of privileged dying
therefore
the walls
the stammering disaffections overcome with lucidity
singing

the great essential pallors
the difficult arisings
the cringing deficits & intonations
it is we who refuse
the core as poisoned kinesis
as divisive cornucopias which operatically strangle
with philosophical pressures ensconced in somatology

not strife throughout rebellious negation
not a plummeted Stygian conclusive
cradled inside a hand written lava

so
to circumvent flow
to contaminate distance

is to merge with stoppage
with mendacious & forthright cellular locales

therefore
one remains closed
threatened by objects
by the oppressive condition
of one life & one body

such perception is a curse
is a demiurgic sun expelling condemned light
from a universal fissure

such is the Occident
with divisions
with turpentine stampeding
with Marx in his later embers
purporting to give us bread
to take our slumber away by harassment

Marx
by way of the Maoists
forcing us into cadres
into productive labour divisions

each unseasonable aridity
they compelled
they sought to lynch us by our teeth with hairs from the Yaks
so as to make us take on character
& cajole our personae with sub-dominate preaching

we as divisibles
as laborious panic
as nausea by stricken adjustment
we were consumed by jarring smells of rugas & omegas
by garish discipline & dysfunction
therefore
indigestible & comprised of breaking points
we were Engels' 'socially necessary labour'
didactic codes against 'surplus value'
we
the pivot of labour within the ordinary fragment
conjoined by Marx
who links the 'complex' with the 'concrete'
& with the butcher Mao condoning the 'peasant associations'
taking 'temples' of 'gods' as a blatant workers' fortress
ritual objects
'piled' into a 'corner'
smashed
the incense burning stifled
ritual performance condemned as pestilence
as lavish & decadent ebullience
the clash between levels of being
beginning
on the twenty-third day of the ninth month of the year of the 'Iron Tiger' *
the Chinese dominance
a skilless & debased eclampsia
a raid on the soul by means of brandished claustrophobia
the cold vicious medium of the cobra
biting us
shocking our celestial monerons into dread
making us collapse in palsy along the trails
shaking with paralytic stupor
under a gas of Marxist cinder crosses

we
who appeared as vague
as transcendental with phobia
became the barbaric members of a blighted morale
a condensed insurrectionary focus of guile
& we who erupted against the Chinese at 'Tsetang' *
& all our ignited venerability burned protective salt into our gauntlets
the resistance
like a force of green bodily integers
summoned from the sun by higher anger & opprobrium
it was we
converging 'on Norbu Lingka' *
part of the '30,000 who defenced all exits'
who
with power
ferociously patrolled the walls
who seized & lynched a 'collaborator at entry'
then
the 'mortar bombs' 'at four ... the following afternoon'
17 March 1959

the 'bombardment' began in the dark early hours
three meridians after the mortars
our hands peeled
our throats blown into rivulets

then the running stench of blood
the tumultuous ruination
by language conveyed in suppurating goitre
convective dolomites hurled as flesh through their targets of materia
the concretism blazing
& the seen & the unseen wandering between themselves as confused
& embittered mirages

here was Marx
here was the State
the inches geared by specific labour & yield
by the 'value' of 'value'
by technic peasant production

for all Mao's peasants were low
despicable
grinding
as the voice of crushed centipedes screeching from a lantern

& this in no way signals our cause
to take up ferocious measuring rain
to savour as our substance anachronistic dialectics

by March 23rd we were bloodily crushed
& given as praxis a life of leper's drills
of future as banquet of sorrow
as threnody
as requiem
as shelter under culpable acids & pain

we of enriched preambles of calm & non-motion
above a blank & imperceptible goddess
we Tibet
we the 'Glorious' suns of 'Learning'
famous for our teachings of the black & 'occult' arts
we
of the '100,000 Sermons' conclude
There has arisen' from the depths the prime illuminator's power
The Maker of Light who gives eyes to the world'
'Gotama'
'out of the miry pit'
who 'stands on dry ground'
The Prince of Physicians'
master of corruption
floating above the mansions of angels transparent with sparks
with unpossessed infinities
Gotama
he who opens life beyond the plentitude of complexity
beyond the deadly perseverance whose name defies the presence
of knavish opium caesuras

we
with top most reverence & honour

with our bloodless wings
with our meditative anthropometry
ensouling our balance
for the 'Judgement of the Dead'

we who breathe through terrible powers of clarity
are able to transmigrate through form
once as a flock of blood pheasants
then as a scale of singing demon fish
we who've ingested spells
from intensive Muru enchanters *
from the monsters of scaly occult ravines
shaping our forms through osmosis
so as to transmute the scope of disaster
we
with our 'Depth of Body'
with our 'Breadth of head'
with our green 'Pharyngeal teeth'

because of such elliptical writhing
we called 'The leading oracles in Lhasa'
'the Nächung' & 'the Karmashar'
the masters
inflamed with clairvoyance from psychic citron ore

& we
Myrmidons of the 'Demon King'
came not as deficits
or as figments of a spare & misleading contagion
but as elements entranced by utter liquid as existence
with preternatural blazings
under kindled smoke
from a fire which formed from doubled cinnabar suns

we
the vortical base
the flammable adherents
here
our diagrams of loneliness go higher

than an Asiatic contour
than a broken interrogation

we
in this magic vessel
await our return to a transparent Lhasa
with its outpouring glare
with its incendiary chalice

we
of the old certitude of mantras
of lucid spell by arising
of incinerate & cascading ritual

it is we who compose on 'slabs'
'of black painted wood'
dusted with chalk & horizons
therefore composed
with blank symbolical scrawlings
risen above
the baneful bullion keepers
fulminate
as a luminous neurology of brilliance

then the senses hover in the deepest interiors of hearing
into musically wafted niveous elevation
tumulose
alpestrine
declivitous
incorruptible
candescent
powerful as to balefire & to plague
as to dense arcana & its ruses

we came to Nächung *
for the solemn principle of learning
so as to live for each of the next substanceless eternities
to spawn confusion as to age
as to the place & time of our private spawning grounds

as to puzzle
crux
rebus
logogriph

we who bowed in dimness
at the throne 'of the great sorcerer'
& 'upon it lay his robes' & 'accoutrements'
'the great sword on the left'
'the magic breastplate' with its fires
the 'great brass cap loaded with gold'
of he who was possessed by the 'ferocious white monster'
with its 'three heads'
with its 'six hands'
atop
an apparitional 'white lion'

attended
by the Tibetan 'King of Battle'
on a 'Wild Yak' & a heinous 'deer'
'whilst over its head' floated 'yellow hatted Lamas'
& he spoke
of a stream without claws
of 'furious bulls'
of negative 'peculation'
as he instinctively proclaimed
'a magic circle'
'a bundle of tents'
'a flag on a sheep's horn'
between
'Black peas'
& 'Indian grains'
this from the sovereign 'Karmashar Magician'

this prophecy given
from the 'doctrine holder'
from the The Bird-headed One'

he warned
of buried transmigration forces
of other voids & other worlds
not under reflective microbes of piercing
or at the punished spawnings within the darkened peaks of Uranian neurosis
but in the cyclonic vapours
in the essential qualities
in the higher cerulean

a non-invasive aquamarine
oblique to the wintery burning system
oblique to the solemn terrestrial enclaves
as a wafting psychic meridian
instantaneous
with the untapped domains of other stellar locales
of runic
explorational hamlets
with its brilliant visual lamas
with its 'Four mythological guardian kings'
he of the 'East'
'white like the dawn'
he of the 'West'
'a glowing red'
& 'the southern guardian'
gold in 'colour'
& over the 'northern realms'
a visage marmoreal with greenness

this the Tibet
of unknown crystallography
of haunted gateway gems
of feral blue demons

Tibet
a massive facade of cold
a 'House of the Gods' effulgent with darkness

what of its Elysiums?
its sulphurs?

its muttering spells?
its purgatorial abasement?

what of its 'butter lamps'?
of its 'Eight Lucky Signs' & 'Glorious Emblems'? *

not vanished
not ossified
but intrinsically transmuted
like a magical coruscation
into neither of the obvious conglomerates

not Saturnian
nor Venusian
nor the stuttering scoria in the Oort dimension
but as bleeding periscopic canals
as in sacrificial flickerings
non-sirenic as in chronicled secular scansion

so here
life follows a syllabus of omens
that populations
hyposthenic & wizened
will fall
without a trace to mark their driftings
therefore
oceans filled with 7 bony diphtherias
with strange nasturtiums expressing their scales & opaqueness
from which
a new lama appears sprung from matchless diphthong cradles
as an unplumbed species of theroid
timeless as the blood of primordial honour
he bears the fruit & the burning
of a merged & nomadic logos
of illusive chaparrals of smoking arsenic & utopia
& his beguiling power of multiples
are the string of lives
are the roundelays of breathing
through era upon unshattered era

through all the brimstone teachings
through all the stridulous impacts
of shaken blood
& soil
& boundary

the Noachian anonyms
lost
burnished with exploded memorials
paying one's way through strife
with fowl or alligator's coinage
we've risen above
the nightmarish gold
the trivial electrums

& we think of Gyges the Lydian *
with his 'rude oval' coinage
of 'Croesus' *
whose 'ten staters of silver equaled one piece of gold'
with the 'daric' of aurous
with the twenty flaming 'siglos' the equal of one 'daric'

or Parthian bronze
or Sassanian silver
all vanished
all culled into a lifeless rock of lunar quiescence
or a deformative lake with shadows of diamond

this
the human era & its guile
with the Asiatic Bullock
with the tiger with its mud scales bleeding
& the tragic sense of danger
throughout destructive ballets
culminate on earth as sinister blood mirages
with its cracking shale
with boiling stars as its orbit

perhaps earth
a faulty lineage habitation
as riddled utterance migration by damaged destiny as cipher
or perhaps
secondary turbulence due to pestiferous compass points as plasma
there is 'riddling'
says the voice
migrations soiled
with demonic plankton
with shaken thermal hallucinations
the divine distinction
marred by lesions
across the moment of the magic birthing channel

the featureless deceptions
the incoming soul
& the signal of its wretched planetary phasmas

so
the earth as voice
as morose medicinal body
as prime calendrical demise

under this jeopardy
we seek for the first expressive hydrogen auroras
for cosmic ancillary winds
for the first true enigmas of fortune
for prolusion
for the grammar of protasis

without bones addressed
without locution emblazoned
we've come to a height
to a magical transmogrific
as if the moon
with its feverish locusts
had turned the tides into darkness
into raging in-clinical stamina

& the earth
now an unstable glade
a dishonoured fraction

& humanity
now refusing its own scales
& the mercury of its own existence

we
in liminal exile
instinctively blessed with sanction from the highest lama
to go further into causes
to open new migration routes
to battle through confrontment

not a spellbound naumachia
or escape by sculpted nautical symbology
but insight across the flaming planetary field
across its deepening necrobiosis
we see
a populous necrology
increased by a tortuous estrangement
by causes unspecified as to exoteric golconda

as to drawn & quartered topologies
as to answer according to numerical compacting
we have no plausibility
no instinctive message to convey
as to the alvine
or the abstract
the nigrescent human field
is like a wayward carbolic
or a venomous predacity
with a less & less refined devolvement

yes
a sporadic gore
a seared consumption

we
of the rimless galaxies
we
of higher electrical intention
not concerned with the sun
or the fatal brew of its deadly 'helium ash'
but with other intensive reading diameters
with other eradications & species springing forth
with new inspired rotation gases

we
who negate the gravid
who summon forces
rapid & oracular with menace

we see the stars
through new calamity & adventure
we who see
with the sudden burst of an emptied luminosity

we exist
voracious with nullity & blankness
we who feast on flames from 'Saint Padma'
on rains from winged 'thunder bolts'

unlike the voice
from moaning burial vaults
we invoke the laloplegic as mantra
as magically soundless baryphony
thriving as we do
in this meteoritic spheroid
which hovers
which suspends itself in 'piercing' 'sapphire' skies
above the 'cinnamon sparrows'
above the 'red-legged crows' & the 'ravens'

unlike
the rough religious hymns
sung throughout 'Western Tibet'

we thrive on lightning
not like volatile monarchs
stuffing ourselves with asps for illusive provocation
nor like the hermits who plunge into wayward in-audia
with their 'rosary bits of human bone'
with their personal goblet cast from various skulls
we are neither of these races
stuttering as they do in chronicles of self-panic
as denial of excess
& excess against denial
none of these forces erode us
nor build from their cacophonies a syndrome
to harass us
or vanquish our seeming aloofness by spell

to the potentates we can say
that you've wasted your demons on envy
& to the ghostly tenants of caves we can say
that yours unless ferocity
is numbed by despotic branches on fire

we
of high magic
of timeless rectitude & cleansing
of fierce immunity & weaving
have burned up resistance
have scattered the laws
have torn down the prophets

we of new migration cycles
we of salt & blank ambrosial growings
of the life of vastitude
of interminate immensity & flying
are un-remitting
continuous
innumerable
undying"

Haiti

> " ... these undistinguished dead become known as that anonymous heritage, les Morts."
> — MAYA DEREN
> *Divine Horsemen: The Living Gods of Haiti*

"We
bubonic
with blackened altering transmissives
with burning nerve length & schisms
twisted in piercing soils
in dark pre-maturity & rage

we the dead
we the pressure & the cyclone of Haiti
savage with usurption
with claustrophobia by scarob
by blood loss & groaning
we who've taken spikes from our entrails
from suns we've had exploded in our nostrils
we who were spawned in harassment
in catastrophic silicate meanderings
in acidic neural complexity

corrupted & slashed
in lightless x-ray vacuums

we who swelter in cold & heatless malachite
in blatant triangle missives
in thoughtless inversion & drought
above burning shells of crab
above a flood of random burial law
like cobras
or gazelles
or eaglets ruined in stunted cemetery icons

it is we who speak
with a sun of splinters spewing from our heart
from our thorax burning with intestinal moray explosion
we
the Africa of Songhai & Mali *
we
of original reptile wisdom
we
the first gatherers of wool
through sun
through apertures spinning
in a ruptured lightning gorge

we
the dead
who blister
who channel poltergeists from lightless peeling rums
as spies

as wild omega charges
beyond ruthless murdering dossiers
beyond the Tontons & their terror *
we float
above abscess torrents
above the bloody belladonnas
& their microbes & their seas
so we emit
lesser bodies of dying
lesser holocaust driftings
therefore we burn
in the bloodless heat of whispers
in stony cloves & disjunctives
in raw botanical monsoons

whenever the crops boil & disease themselves as acid
there is malaria by forgery
starvation under gemstone
as if treachery had been launched
throughout a shadow of bodies

throughout the reign of ominous modernity
where we shift between sulphur & limbo
between plaintive spillage & body
because
there is a discourse of bodies
of chaparral by misnomer
of splendiferous mirage
& blistering anti-edict

we the dead
transcripting ruin & vapour
with demonish lisping trot
with salvos
by diorama & plague
by the very principle of pain
split apart & cyclonic

as for the souls of our two former killers
Papa Doc
with his rotted & greenish blood
with his consort
the Madame
ailing in her rubies & bones
we accuse them
with every quarter of their accursed mandibles
with every despicable vibration as owls
their gestures
their veins as leopards turned around in a mirror
grown from themselves lashing out as monsters

we see them now
throughout a wrenching prolapse through the kingdoms of hell
caged by the demons
within the macerated bones of mutual self-bleeding

she
in lacerated sullage
he
atop

her fly infested vulva
like a gargoyle
squandered in the wax of his miserable finality

our demarcated vultures
we send as drones of heat to their cage
as fabulous syphilitics
as arrowed curses in French
we
of course
as witness
in electric timing Bermudas
in nux vomica & braille
in tense volitional compound
view the two monsters
linked by spittle & voltage
by poisoned hummingbird's refrains
drawn by the flame of a flawless nautical violence
headlong with villainy
with saw tooth roses & blood
we come to them
with our vulturous drones
shrieking
mocking the Tontons with their terror
glaring
at what we call the gargoyle couple
with bursts of colourful threatening damnation

we illuminate their minds with memories of the Tontons
'with their long curved machetes' *
up 'Avenue John Paul II'
striding through
'Rue Martin Luther King'
by swinging axes at their eyelids
seeing the marching henchmen reflected in the blades
the gargoyle couple
forced to watch their own contusions
with post-infernal piacular dysgenic
where they live as new Avernals

under our special burst of watchfulness
under a billion glinting razors
their death is quantified
partakes of astro-physicality
is wound by wound in saturated edges

we
the dead
send against them plankton armies
empowered by anger with a special knowledge of torture
perhaps an eye taken out & put back at angles
or having the teeth tragically spilled into an open rectal furnace
this is the law that the vultures instinctively sculpt for us
we who transmit wounds from our higher squalor of dying
we
with the sunrise anaemia
with the rust endured emulsion rains

yes
a sun obscured by ravens & pulleys
by locusts in vents
by drafts of defunctive water beetles

& so dawn
for the frightened gargoyle couple
fanatically suspended
marred
monomial with ruses & flailing
with hints of viridian marking their blood
glaring
scorching & freezing
their bony ruminations
their darkened mineral excitement
under scalpels of a bilious stony catalytic
enveined
by 'hum bars'
& cacti
& 'static'
& 'noises'

this couple
coiled by lava as adhesive
by moral flames & lisping

the bankrupt mechanics of compromise
can never be equated
with their broken form
with their scorched acetylene howling

you can see we have a certain quantity of zeal
of frenzy turned over & spewed out as sulphur
as rope of metal kilowatts drilled into the optics

this is the gargoyle couple
living by torture
by each excruciating mental fatality
that they've rapturously inflicted
all the suffering returning like blackened starlight in their mouths
according to the vultures
each limb sawn off & eaten
each monument they've built
plummage by scarification
& by their rancid emulation
they suffer from trichinosis & spasms
rending themselves with imaginal centaur tramplings
with ancillary bursts
with neo-scorpion gargantua

& the cage we've made
corrosive with electrons & shadow
shattered
& magically held aloft by venomous aphid's predation
by meandering vampire mirages
& the gargoyle couple
mere trodden upon enclitics
who've lost the stress of their pouring murderer's grammar
their existence contracts into a question of hives
of fiery burrowing worms
encomiastic with forms

a eulogy for sickened blood begetters
compressed with ringworm salt
with bursts of dorsal acid

the enchorial darkness of Haiti
obliquely littered with bone chips & sternums
scattered across beaches
in the high errata of shifting property & wool
European
with its pre-figured deadliness
with its nail studded whipping boards
with its flaming histiography buried in sunless fishing huts
'burned with boiling cane'
'manacled & smeared with molasses'

a patient chronicle of rot
whose disease infested botflies swagger
with the brutish persistence of rape
equated by a gryphon's congealed disfigurement

then
the abruptly stolen rums
freed by new Dahomean incarnation
by suicides which strengthen

under Mackandal there manoeuvred a death broth *
by poisoning the slavers' dietary juices
we forced the invaders to view themselves
in mirrors of raging voudou bells

it was cult as demonstrative anger
as vicious unstinting sub-plot
we who terrorized the grafting pots
of the funnels of heat as they spilled into iron

this is our history
with ferocious radices & pollen
across remorseless flotillas of anguish
the solemn complex of general weight & connivance

under bluish medical neurosis
growing our spare teeth to enunciate barbarity
then to take up a fleshless opium counting
by the power of intrigue & breathing
this was our reasoning
as if floating on a raft of livid sea iguanas
across a series of pauseless parasitical enticements
empowered by storks inside an arachnoidal beehive

we've splintered our cysts
into wayward tombstone phonetics
into synthetic kilogram
into tainted kindling exposure

such intransigence being no more than a mode
of nursing a spring of fabulous personal vipers
amidst oedemas of collapsing vitrescence

as eerie citizens who burn
in the dense morbidity of monads & frustration
we
the first inhabitants of runic leper's preambles
who scrawl on blazing diadems with allopathic fusions
give to the deadly gargoyle couple
strontium blessed with arsenic & nickel

we
the dead
combined with ferocious Petro murmurs *
with strong ballistical gall
with a riddled lightning forge as our map
burning
with a matchless in-sonority
with large physical proofs
like filtering a lamp with oil in a zealous lion's oasis
we
hacked with machetes
stabbed in the eyes with crystallized assault
cease to be imported

tangled
spat upon
cast in the vapours with impunity

so we've granted ourselves this law
that we watch the gargoyle couple from our vector
as we vote & restructure new methods of torture

ah
as one mulatto has put it
'let us inject a powerful yaws into their skulls & make bite at
    [indelicate cloves
while licking at the flames of darkness'

'let us stir up with our pain
imaginary serpents & scorpions
full of rot & metaphysical tumult
so that the gargoyle couple

stammers with seismic kinetics'
so says our brother
who was hanged in the streets
despite the depth of his marvellous Nubian rigour

so we
separate & as one
with our blazing salamander's slaver
with our courage blown up & regained
in the wrath of this limbo
we burn the symbols in this zone
we make up the acreage
we infest the soil
with the burden of raw faeces
taking on the power
of casting suns on a chart
beneath a river of dice & sharks
we
who even gamble in death
who furtively lengthen each flowing river of pathology

dazzled with blindness
Greek with locomotive infection

Simone
with her torrential voudou blisters
hatching oracular mental plunder
her veins freshly lit with inversion
with her bloodthirsty lover Luckner Cambronne *
circling her sores like a disjunctive bat
attempting to vilify François with a magically conjured army of crabs

we
who neutralize our rivalry
we who stare with the power of maimed aphotics

therefore
the gargoyle couple
forced by tubercular concision
to expose themselves
to we
the dead
in their cage of writhing mongoose innards
placing splinters in their nostrils
with nourishing milk out of reach

we have given them the fact of a pliable sensation
we who've sculpted vultures to attack their eyelids
to suck & maniacally harvest their blood
we who exist as voice
as vociferant limbo & danger
we who profit from nerves
from a strangeness which strategizes muscles
which sickens
& burns
like the fate of strangled hunting geese
flying from bluish mirrors & salt

for above the cage are malificent auroras
auroras which strengthen
like hieroglyphics which emblazon

therefore
we maximize frustration
we haunt the gargoyle couple with a puncturing kind of guilt
with the fact of crimson hummingbird faeces
where the vultures
whirring above the aura of their skulls
emit from their shrieks didactic cadavers as a tense form of plasma
& they appear
& we empower their actions
to moan with debility
to hiss with great reaction
so that the cage is further stunted
with a deeper
more intrusive disquiet

we whose arms are nettles of kinetic solstice grains & wattage
whose end was untimely signed
whose suns were thwarted without the nuance of vapour
are parabolas of urine
are strangers of molten
whose alphabetic eye is noose to old volcanoes & lizards

in the salt of the guillotine manger
we
with the incest groans
with the matchstick howls
are precarious
are ruthless
are bled upon

we who exist
as ransomed cobalt abysmals
who live & die in structured silicate pontoons
which explode & regather as spectacular pumice
we who exist as a scar
of eternal & murky significance
in this crepuscular enclave
like a wasp
or a windless brandishing torch
or a planet at dusk whose rotation is suspended in evil

we are honed by our dread
we burn & we drift
as a blank & a-rhythmic burst by witness
in blind meridian burrows
fraught by internal nigrescence & terror
the extremities
the mud leeches
the flameless underwater dartings
ruled in synecdoche by a harried nomadology
by monsoon & clinging as our only grasp of fire

this
the ironies of malevolent Stygian rest
greenish
beneath corroded gypsum flames
as medicines or ointments
or floating sand iguanas
we exist as nutrients
as hotly lettered moths
as a flock of magnetic whistling pediculates
climbing to a peak of imagined rhythmical snow
near the first seven burnings of elliptic proto-suns
therefore
we are deaf with irascence
with monomial ice & tearing
we who have counted our mazes by death clocks
by brutal cyanide potions
by mixed centripetal blasts
by the bladder of vultures & gender
we who exist as lost theocracy & arrogance
as a green reactive sub-base
it is we
who blister our songs in the flagrant treachery of exile
it is we
who don ourselves in dripping viper's teeth
it is we
who wade in the hair of writhing snakes & sibyls
scorching ourselves in Neptune molten
in twisted citron flamings

yes
we exist
with the pure emotion of hatred
with our riddles & our brine
with obscure & melted needles
we listen with clair-audience
as carnivores
as listless & negative dust authority

for us
the living who are forced to peruse us
hear us with superior molecular tragedy
for every dawn they come near us
for every strife that they fear
we acknowledge their scorn & ruin
with muzzles
with dejection & hopeless bread
soaked with a sorrowful screaming
because we know that our vocal omniscience exists
that we flagellate & kindle in the first scorched immensity
in the first soulless terror
riddled
bloodless
dreaded
under the vines
of a morose & circular vector
contradicting all the pattern
all the physics of vein & law

& we
of dazzling sunless invictas
of the stony looking glass indictments
like a fetish
or an ice mirage
or inconvivial herrings
anointed with plasma & darting

we
who have surmounted

the formal foundations of steam
who have taken
the first formal step of leech against leech
against the restless nerves of these gargoyle personas

first
a hot & unglistening wax
flung down the slopes of their temples
then the implantation of leeching sewers in the mounts of their throats
our alchemical understanding
to distil transparency from their sufferings
their heritage of stains
their winged & in-aerial stumbling in faeces
their grotesquely spun inertia imprisoning their compounds
in blinding pulmonary thickets
in procedures dissected on burning chromium tables
near the crest of intensive scalpular gyrals
their wounds
stitched & re-stitched
with a calibrated voltage

François *
Simone *
you exist at our behest
if we want your flesh to slither
or have your eyes extracted in fragments
it is the measure of our bedazzlement with anger
drowning your arms in potent urines & metals
we declare with the power of triangular ciphers
that we remain

invective
vengeful
classic
sailing with trees across a harbour of blood
intoning with cupidity & honour
with the blows of erratic Python rounds
this is exposure François
the country of liquid

the buried oracular demons
therefore
under the sun of Lawrencium or Ytterbium
we have brought to bear
elenctic reasoning by utterance

were you
'armed'
'hooded'
smashing down the door of the beautiful Yvonne Rimpel?

do you know her François
'Yvonne Rimpel' *
'Yvonne Hakime Rimpel'
'Yvonne' in 'slippers' & nightgown
'pushed' in a 'car' & driven away
to the 'rural suburb of Delmas'?

do you know her François
she who "counted nine" of you
who stripped her
& began to rape her

with the beating being so brutal she faded in and out of awareness
bullets whizzing by her skull
'her naked body'
'kicked in a trench'?

are your aware of this François
was your presence included
with the nasal invective
to 'finish her off'
because their family had upstaged you?
were you protectively aggressive
like a palpitating cheetah
chewing on citrus & oblivion?

these are bony questions François

for instance:
did you savagely dispose of opposition in Bel-Air? *
'foul smelling Bel-Air'
Port-au-Princes'
oldest
poorest
most massive opposition?

were you guilty of culpable heresy?
by one assaultive strain after another?

we can say that their thoughts of axial in-melodias
you sought to crush
to destructively behead

so therefore
was your hand exposed in this massacre of sulphur?
in this larceny & massacre through sewage?

we want to know François
was their hunger assuaged by populous drill bits & caffeine?
by sugar dipped in rattles & methane?

was it your conscious intent
to keep their hunger at scorching decibels
compounded by a daily visual wrath?

by faecally stained woods?
by tileless emasculated cooking dioramas?

what of the urine François?
of the tubercular eyes?
of the rickets rampant with 'curvature' of the spine?

of loss of minerals in the bone?
of dense bodily contraction & fever?
these being the deficits that we question François

& what of the Bel-Air that you knew
with its scabs
with its embrangling locust armies

where shortly after your bleak ascendence
you ordered murder
you ordered 'cargoes'
of men & women & beasts
'gagged with rags'
'immobilized with ropes'
their bodies pushed into an undried gorge of indifferent cement
'protesting wildly'
like a fractious & broken carcass
dark & blankly sordid
in a 'defecating' fear
their tomb ensconced
beneath an 'old wooden cross'

is the description not correct?
is the analysis impure?

here
your harnessed satanic guile was active
brazen
with a gullible intensity

in contradistinction
our volatile anguish is rising to a pitch of unspared power
which strengthens itself like many meteors whirling across a
    [sulphurous deluge
our force being gained
by a black heptagonal anger
we who exist
in syllogistic absorption
blazing
tending to count our incitement with precarious disorder
by means of tense & nomadic authority
no longer writhing as tragic contemplatives
as spores in darkened butchering stalls

each trauma
each despicable kinetic
we savagely ascribe to your presence as it flickers
jailed behind your fissioning radium bars François
of course
this is not the mathematics of carious & axial abstraction
nor the sleet of a picturesque candelabra spinning
drastically modelled by the tincture of squab
we are concerned with wounds François
with the deadly & unachievable torment which ruins

in these stages of utter oblivion
it is we the deadly messengers
of this first utopian Armageddon
in this first impermanent claustrophobia of demise
where we challenge you François
doubled over in blinding
with the body of Simone
your necks phantasmagorically scorched
with a series of sundogs & vipers
with a chemically forged hyena's daring
to place a mark upon your ribs from its scorching
brewing from our warlock's hive a scent between your mouths
for permanent arousal & hounding
throughout the involuntary statute of your surcease

so we ascribe to your deeds as Haitians
as a colony lit by in-seasonal salt & blood
as depicted by the force inside the agony of herons
placing inside your washing items monomial grafts & spleen
the microbes you breathe carcinogenic phonemics
so that flares from the Icarian Sea
become the metempsychosis of shrapnel & shark bite
from dazzled Iberian bleeding come sores
this being
our gift to you François
from explosive annulment & congestion
from refined & deadly aerial lobotomies
raised from the treachery of kilns

from the harried measures of an ox blow
we give you thankless & squared fertility phantoms
a glossolalia by core
by rootless exile & concision
giving you proof by psychic incest & worm
therefore
above static radium cage
there is a lightless singing simian dove
niveous
appearing above the vultures with its specific inclusion of moaning
haunting the flames with a shattered resonance in both your spines
yes
your groans
the pall of your trenchant miasmas
plutonic with a depth of convulsion

therefore
a crude millennial intercourse in stone
repeated as horror ad-infinitum

& your offspring
accrued by damnation
chewing on scorpions
on newt en-waxed lactose
we think of 'chubby six year old Jean-Claude'
eating 'mounds' of thick 'spiced' 'ham' delectables
his genetic direction
in raw in-commensurate oozing
attempting to lean
upon his calculated staff of dark incapable arrogance
sired beneath a sign of garish esurience
smitten
with the callous unbreakable law of the spineless
so therefore François
we have named a weakness in your flank
a suture of oil in your cassock
erupting from your bone valves a splintered proto-torture

& Simone
you old spasmodic wailing princess
splayed & re-sutured by spells
in your stumbling ark of richocheted erratums

in your forced & eternal coupling without letup
you crave for endless caesuras
for interregnums filled with concealment

this
we cannot grant you
weary with demonic bleeding
weary from the carriage of skulls which surrounds you
the overbearing diablos in your spillage
& the sneering carrion poachers which possess you
& ring your nerves like tensors with brewing phantoms of gall
it is you Simone
in the depths of this irony of coupling
tortured in the zone of this joyless compensation
with François
who eats you with his thirsting
like a nightmarish clockwork
or a disaster blown from the rhyming of omens

as you inflict Simone
why François? why the gullible vacuum of Haiti?
why the spoils of its motionless voudou?

we answer with thievery
with gross invidious murder
emitted from your throne room

so
you are forced to couple for eternity
the sperm inside your womb
like a spate of chiselled branches
painful
fading in & out of your zone of bleeding
unlike the pleasurous flows of Faustina *
your haemochromes splatter

& your flanks become as raw as a salivous lava
embedded with stolen glass
with ominous threats speeding throughout your bodily chain
therefore
your eyes exist as no more than vipers
as no more than the Loch Ness symbology
fetid
like a smouldering set of ruses exponentially embrangling

& François
exploding in her flesh
with the power of spiders' burins
constantly pumping blood through a desert of shrunken arteries
like galactic trichinosis
causing nausea & swelling disorders
seeing yourself François
as in the blaze of an English jailhouse
your shadow captured in jaundiced abatement
as if to hold off a culminating incalescence
as if to let us spy on your attrition
punished at the core by a blistering obscenity
it's as if we saw you François
with your night gown opened in public
with your tangled paws on rancid nesting grates

& we think of your loins as transported bleeding
as the reddish leakage of canine
with greenish boils that explode
therefore
you eat
& plough

& smell each other's offal
as if arisen from the literature of ghouls
unlike Maturin or Walpole *
there is the cataclysmic test
within this smoky hall
of the judgement of the dead

Kaleidoscopic Omniscience

& you François
who greeted the musicologist Courlander *
'in a black woollen suit'
your eyeballs lit by the flickering logic of candles
& your graceless ozone
mute
dour
with the dire absurdity of a fresco in darkness

this was your lot
to mix your arrogance with terror
your hallucination with hounding
therefore
we surround you with pauses
with susurrations that glimmer
that make diamonds burn
with crushing dislodgement
like the cowering cook as portrayed by Petronius *
we howl at the scarlet misery of your debasement
like the sniping of skuas
or the lapping at your face with the tongue of a dragon

therefore François
we are cannibals by the fact of incitement
by soulless signalling mangoes flying from graves
& we exist
as a cruel & tenacious credit
we are reindeer movement across wild intuitive mud coasts
our memoirs exhausted
our former lives assessed as valueless dogs at birth
suffering from contagions
this being the way that our heritage was brokered
was conceived as in-vitality
on par with the sounds as derived from ranaria
multiple with gargantua & darkness

your cage inflames us
with a higher surmounting of hatred
burning your powers
in the fire of old Venusian eaglets

therefore
we command
that you break her François
then braid her bones with pliers
so that she drown & revives
with cold insomnial screaming

with the effort we command
you know how Sisyphus scowled with his efforts half broken
in glare
a lean testimonial by clinging

since the thesis of your motion is rape
atop your gargoyle bride
in the praxis of this 'grim regime'

you
who placated Castro *
with pardons
with terrible cowardice
with plates of bone as gifts

then just as quickly
you turned by mean convenience
to American principle policy
squealing like a deadly bureaucrat gone bad
& got the bastard's reward of guns & connivance
by feigning a high morality
protecting angels from the snares of Marxist edification
you
a dried up virgin
eclipsed in gryphon's armour
structuring an ism
to play the role of saviour
of the one recorded monster who enlightened

the one self hurtled onto uranian inversion
who scribbled your bone on ignominious parchment
the letters

the charred microbial sails
their soundless destiny as raven
their sonar of nails by frustration

this was the suddenness
the glazed abandonment in your eyes
in your death enshrouded poses
by fright
& the amperage of coffins

& the scarred domains of your oblivious dominance
imbued with scurrilous pandemonium
& we
of arthritic *ignotas*
cursing
singing our souls to death over spleen
the difference being
we of utopian potentia
we of the first blinding ice fields
reborn in the avicular
above the focused snares of lower holocaust models
not as owls
or voided emus in crystal
we live in this mingling potentia
watching your nostrils flare with empty novocaine & gasping
attempting to breed in this catapult of stifling
upon waves of remorseless hellebore seas

because our potentia has grown
we dismiss our exposure
to the isle of Tortuga *
to the Matheux mountains *
or to the city of Jérémie *
or to the waters of Port Salut *
our unknown poltergeists as ferrets

this fire no longer completely contains us

our vibration glistens & has stolen the rays
from a charred & listless panic
mounted by your ilk

we watch with succulence your horror taking shape
as your sullen interior writhing ensues
beneath the half signs of smoke

you have arrived in the city of dungeons
in a zone of lifeless declension
impairment & reversion the general arrows of your names
these are our obstinate leanings
our crouching by-pass determinants

fiends
Demogorgons
selvas with memories

we of Damballah Oueddo *
we of the 'worship of the beautiful in nature'
inclined through these moments
to the powers of Baron Samedi *
of sinister Congolese encroachment mixed with Dahomean Rada *

we
of the high skills of sun
watch you

without letup
having the vultures poke irons in your face
so as to probe your soul for possession
searching for the breech in your tainted labouring eclipses
so as to pull down baskets of fangs onto your livers
so as to bleed & retain the in-convivial
in your smoky solstice mirrors

you are massed with Simone
as in Signorell's 'Condemned' *
your minds

like cold cadaverous iguanodons
sullied at the fount of the teeth
immersed in eruptive monsoons

as carnivores
we force you with sudden starvation
with your bodily ballasts back & forth
in the agony of a blank & zoneless repetition

each hardened caress
a colossus of raw in-cherubic Zoroasters

therefore
we beam François
glowing with diabolical ingratitude
our fortress of ratsbane
fleeting to the Gods
like a gull in amorphic recession

we
gazing on your heated radium isle
as Simone screams with both her tibias cracked open
her acids erupting
her muscles congealed in Pompeian tufa
her hide scraped from spun in-sensory fields
grieving from the loss of her motionless engenderment
burning in a bed of lighted butcher's grease

here involves the fate of your disgraceful biographies

the tongues ripped open & slaughtered
the skulls displayed across a marquee of bitterness

now you are thoroughly wakeless Simone
in your manipulated voudou
where your cherished persona is now threaded with curses
where your envy now blazes as a snarling dopplegänger
    [as an invincible Lorelei
which both dazzles & heightens your crippling astringency

the fatal squab in your tissue
which you recklessly sought to copy in your motives
so that your essence was voided
like a wavering oracular in-density

& the boulevards you witnessed
became an unclaimed errata
a tenacious kind of carking as a brazen set of symbols

so in the presidential palace
you tore into your psyche with less & less assurance
with a vacillating grimness
as to the foils of your previous connivings
as to your rotted denouements
as to your moral loss & writhing

now you are firmly marked
with a crass diphtherial utterance
as if your flanks were burning hooves
on the sands of a pointless potassium

therefore Madame
we note the primeval mockeries
the ill-begotten assassin's revels

yes
the both of you coupling in guilt
around the diphthong tunnels of your assassinated rectums

& we watch
not from erotic candescence
but to further agonize your snares around a suppurating wantonness

our most basic emotion
is simple revenge
to intensify your horror
to watch your labouring blisters burst
throughout your strange coupling for eternity

to watch the two of you riveted
in dense oregano & discomfort

it pleases us to see you
seasoned in distortion
cacophonous
in the very flames of a thriving harassment
tearing & refilling your innards with molten
so that all services you rendered as rulers
are of a permanent & unyielding record

not simply a wake Madame
but soulless irreparable tragedy

as to butchery
let us recollect the corpse of Eric Brièrre *

'a young mulatto'
under torture so gruesome
the majors backed off with vomit
when forced to assemble the corpse

in contrast Madame
though gaunt in office
you've grown ironically corpulent
amidst the sweltering inversions of hell
at the flank of your eyes
demonstrative by spasm
by smoking acrimonious acridine

because
it was your eyes
which witnessed
the would-be usuper Laracque *

you witnessed
his 'stinking' 'bloated' 'fly-infested corpse'
'propped in a chair'
beneath an ironical 'sign saying'
'Welcome to Haiti'

not agrobiology or fate
but the despotic intention of your intimadator's Drachmas

for all the linen in your palace
was singed with the odours of blood
& unlike the catamenial
it was blood designed within boundary
you being psychically in league
with the obese Macoute Sanette Balmir *
who spliced the void with her murderous montage
with her cult of salt & fever
with her negative edicts of brine

from her fierce dialectical pontoons
she reduced her victims to microbial carbon
to a bony & shelless fate
more polluted than an Emperor
carving on carnage

she brought to your impassive probe Madame
wires
in-canonical accents
which empowered your bleeding eyes with strength

& even when François denounced you
there was the toneless marionette in your aura
which absorbed & deafened the crises
& nevertheless consumed the eruptive poltergeist about it

the ambitious greed
the folly to consume
etched into the code of your sprawling salivation

Simone
our fate has granted us vision
that you died at the fissioning of François
that you have joined us in this Gehenna *
in this holographic of flames
in this darkened metaphysic of exile

when describing you
we think of the ferocious she-devil below the 'lower mesopelagic' *
like a vampire
destroying the organs of the male

he becomes a simple source of sperm
his blood
imported from her veins

& you
as counterpoint François
as Omosudis lowei *
a predacious fish with a 'powerful bite'
eating oversized prey with its widely hinged jaw
thus
both of you are doubled as deadly egg & sperm
like sudden aeroliths from infernos
falling into your wretched gargoyle frenzy

we provide for both your intakes
stromy letters of treason
which provides dark condition
with moving elements of twilight
your insistence is now pathetic

as to retreat
we've lost the measure of such tenor
we only think of the 'sleek brown rats'
which crawl through Fort Dimanche *
across the throats of the prisoners
symbolized
by the robbery of jade
under vectors of false & transposed bullion

as your coupled stench ensues
we know the cavernous depths of your lying
as you clenched between your teeth

a catalogue of emeralds & china
now no more than soiled & profoundly channelled vinegars

each brazen amplitude
each furtive spire of razors
you chose François
as methods of ordination
of bleached & vituperative mineral blight
a language engendered under jaundiced meteoritics
constructed from insult
from traitorous & plaintive self-bribery
you took your list of wounds from paved incarceration
from a world dimension forged from the logic of a disabled wooing
redolent with crawling maniacal grubs
you kept at your call the Tontons
horrendous
vicarious
deadly
on par with the German SS or the Croatian Ustashi *
having eyes put out by lightning
or having babies invaded with the thrust of bayonets

it is to you François that we owe this honour
this business of relentless coffin trading
keeping around you
a raft of scabrous animals
brackish
ridden with envy
with sweltering storms of graft

we think
of Luckner Cambronne lover of your unrelenting Simone
peddler of Haitian blood
with his constant supply of corpses shipped to the North
    [for exorbitant levy

just think François
all for profit
the 'broken heads'

the inclement flesh
this
the Haitian frontier
with its all consuming ministry of death

we recall our bodies being flung
into the Gulf of Gonâve *
into infected symmetricals
where the earth would cook the flesh in either diorite or plankton

we
who were forced to draw life from rotational impurities
from the despicable light of a sun forced to shine in its secreta

we come to you François
as a fouled & broken harrier ray
working against your zeal with the power of a hellish metronome
empowered by the wiles of a darkened old Samedi

this is the heightened power of our strife

the wails
the screamings
the blade against blade

we
the dead
who once pleaded for vision
now by the means of vultures
carry acid to your torments
so that your predatory stupor
reveals a strange tubercular seizing neurosis
retching
a dry sheaf of wolves
a swamp of damp circuitous tigers' haemic

yes
we've given you blistered sonar
we've trespassed your lightning & fury

so as to maintain those monstrous ions
returned to your old man's throne room bleeding

yes
we remember carnivorous twitching
at the murder of one Lucette Lafontant *
one breast sliced off
with you observing
the gruesome master of extinction
shaking joyfully from her agony
as an estranged binocular wolf with the skin of frozen pancreas adders

with your painful bufferless arthritics
holding both hands on the death ship
with a scowl transfixed in gratuitous grimace
watching
always watching
with a sweating scalpel & venom

you
who craved the immortal within the light of twisted agronomies
the abandoned farms
the 'imported foods'
giving rise to gullies in the land
to raw mosquitos in the soul
the world of warped intestinal hounding
& the people
drifting from misery to misery
like a cloud with interior monsoon virus
this was your keepsake François
the weird & topical befoulment that you rendered
the zodiac that you grew & peopled with despair

you
who stole from suns
with the thrice rendered dead
who issued cold & putrid phasmas for your lineage
poised around your rancid death incisors
your dense & cretinous rupture gates

the way you rode the corpse Jumelle *
attempting to eat the rums from his ethers

to take the life from his powers
from his high unmurdered prowess
you sought the sap from his swollen fingers
then sought from his magnetic vermin
a windless voudou greed
an exploded succubine soup

certainly not a packet of green & Scottish scenery
or a countryside teeming with a dawn enriched by amber
no
the double sign of secrecy & mobs
of feigned exteriors by a practical kind of quiet

you
in the flesh
like a cataclysmic owl
with dark provocation by stance
by negative sums
by terrifying panics
with your bold & terrible policies by anguish

it is you François
who tore the chains from the demons
in the 'cave called Trou Foban' *

it was you who evoked cholera on the one hand
& seedless dying on the other

the collective was scorched with flameless niacin icing
with the tedious grief of a rambling molten surveillance
surveyed
in a primitive glass pot of ultramarine brutality

yes François
a brace of 'lower magical powers'
an onerous swine investment

& each impeccably engendered crime
was spawned with the soul of devious obsolescence

it was as if your movements were invoked to cast spells
to mesmerize bells by debacle
as with the blasphemous wire to Abel Jérome *
to save the Sansaricq family already murdered *

let us intuit your portrait at the time
with your dressing gown drowned
by your raven & deadly murdering plans

& all your comrades grim
dazzled by an absolute spoilage
screaking like panicked geese
from one site of massacre to another
dupes
who in the cruelty of movement
forgot the depths of their own necrosis

so now we can dwell on our electrocuted whispers

& we command you
to break her François
make her back snap back at the sum of its edges
make her groan with such a sprawling
that you take into account the rotted mange of unworkable dichotomies

you are
the blank embattled goblin
the scar
the village rooster with its skull hacked to pieces in a vat

because you cannot die
you are face to face
with Simone & her harrowing caustics
this metempiric passage
arrested in place
milked from dialectical calumny

we see this
enriched by perfect sonar & glycerin
by clear propensity & innocence

not by prior or omniscient judgement
but by insight
by rise from the depth of alchemical *nigredo*
evolving rhythms
from riveted colonic stains & traumas
lit by the fact of intensive clepsydras

we who were thrust into lifeless inequity
as a maimed design in Moorish gravel
not as inconsequents
or as blank remorseful alloys
but living analogues of mystery
we
who've overcome extinction
who've destroyed your dastardly interim rule
who've erased in-circular motive & bribery

we speak
as the referential poltergeist
as the living comprehension of phasmas ingesting a raving
perjury & ridicule

François
Simone
we of the most heinous of stamina
we of the fire of black anathema berries
passing upon you judgement
at the blind Armageddon you've insidiously arrived at
with its bartered tarantulas
with its wolverine proposals
with its tools in the mist of a post-mortem acid

for in life
there was lying François
always the lying

with your 'Catechism' *
with your 'Breviary' *
books
invested with a shrill & carnivorous mendacity

in the 'Catechism'
you called yourself
' ... Dessalines ... for life...'
in The Class Problem ... of Haiti'
you even spoke
of the honesty of the mind
of Haiti's incessant tragedy
prior to your stealth & your mayhem
now we ogle your fate in the light of your former reports

in the heat of your lightless radium cage
listless
forced to act with furious primary rote
pumping
insistently pumping Simone
with her deadly gargoyle chancres
with her bleak vaginal stone & filth
like burned German arteries
or ancient culpable menses
rooted in noxious stammering & squalor

yes Simone
we speak of you as would a recondite painter
in front of scurrilous hedges

we
with our prosthetic vultures
atop branches of reptilian centigrade
watching
always watching

not to swoop down & tear
at your Teutonic musculatures of stoniness
but psychically to infect your recuperative palette

as the monster without letup surmounts you
with his ungracious function
from the webs of his decimated grainery

we
the disguised
the unsalted
the un-brandable

we've emerged with vigour in this liminal alluvium
in the fumes of this ground up millet
as active runic auroras
as the sun of kindled vampire hamlets

we exist
as other bodies of oxygen
like a collective force
of burning ink & kings

we record
this staggered gargoyle embrace
like poisoned moonrise from mirrors
at the nocturnal cross-roads
we as wise & objective as Ghede *
as 'greatest' of 'healers'
as 'final appeal against death'

so we say to you Duvaliers
we have condemned your memoirs to the fraction of death camp goblets
to dense & regimenting functional devices
your scrolls being blighted by old collaborator's venom
with your insecticidal Tontons
with your extorted blood combines for profit

you
in the splash of prone vermiculate vomits
quaking like thieves under sonar
under gross in-vitality & deadliness

our egregious disregard for chronological surcease
for bodiless wavering
for proselytized infirmity

therefore we clearly speak
beyond neutered ambush bondage
as wild ozonal lepers
with lucid accuracy in our mumblings

we stare
so as to dole out degrees of cosmic measuring torment
as savagely vile volitional veracity

this is vivacity
in its relentless diurnal blackness
in its torched in-secular avernal *nigredo*
a *nigredo* divorced

from any consubstantiation
from any turpitude as worship

so
we invade your tracheas with worms
with soured & depopulated swine

therefore
to resurrect your forms in a govi *
to debate your moral claims in vermilion
is shattered & uplifted travesty by claim

as intuitive vector no cloud beguiles us
no measure haunts us
this as regards your stunted necromancer's voices

as general voice of the dead
we reserve the right to impale your repulsive integuments
with pikes
to swarm your souls with glassy hummingbird's arrows
of course

it is we who have transmuted this hell
who have spun its repetitious arcanums
with strange messianic cadavers
whose voice proclaims a music
of winding jugular torments
of suddenly burning moons
exacting a wrath from any right of reclamation

yes
innovation in the after-life
more colourful pinnacles of opprobrious honing & starvation
for this is the thirst François of your fetid rat en-vigoured bones
of the roubles you sought to store in your liver
because now
with Simone
you are collective lamprey sparks
germinal dissonance

fire
with burning letters in treacherous exfoliation

being has turned on you François
it has shaped the pellets from your darkened gargoyle staring
as a roofless marquee
corroded
the radium
leaking through your plaintive decibel connivance
hoping for a sound of neutered Calliopes
so as to give Simone
an advantage of ballistical turpentine

Simone & François
equally spat upon & haunted
more than having mental perforations
or the uttered fact of a treeless ideal
you are possessed
by this permanent declension
by this utterly intangible sundering

as a dire fort
in a blistering vacuum
we've summoned
a definitive nomadology
we've shaken loose stasis
we've opened up squalls inside a faultless heavenly rotation

as to the old inclined movement of alternate heavens & bodies
we've reversed the cycle
we've suspended the charge

we've implanted your stasis inside a blank & definite oration
like a portfolio in abscess
in this dimly shadowed gargoyle arraignment
because we've weighed your auricles
in response to riddled cadmium gauntlets
because your mixtures have failed
& will never know the haunts of higher watery confusion
will never know an inkled a-priori
or hear the bell that rings from the throne of a higher solar magnetics
this you will never know
with your foul piacular cunnings
with the halo inside your double hell born reactions
beneath your smashed sarcophagi of prongs
there is an academic blizzard
as if you handled your ghastly ledgers
by chromatology & meters
by false chatoyant counting skills

how many mulattos to be murdered in this Vesper?
how many votes against this or that vernacular?

who are the deformed & atramentous conquistadors?
who are recruits for wind-swept malediction & disappearance?

these were the questions of your transposed gases
these were the thoughts in your garrison of dioxide

now
as holographic gargoyles
as reptilian sheets without countable transparency
there is a need to plunge a stave in your ribs
to bring forth arguable vermin

& so
the homology we describe
is your presence existing as infected abstentia

'two dog hookworms'
'aberrant' infections
'creeping' eruptions

'serpiginous tunnels in the skin
caused by migrations of larvae'
the result
a 'cubic centimetre of blood' in 'a day'

this
the non-existent ambulation
of 'fatigue'

of 'dullness'
of 'apathy'
of 'melancholia'

we exist in the fully operative cannibal's priority
in the broken alembic which hisses
therefore
we play with the cold
with the haunted thermal *australis*
like the tense unforgettable mystery
in poisoned bird-like kelp
equating the tides of heat
as endless noctambulous lustrums

& our utterance
as exaggerated will

as balanced & traceable stasis
floats with a cosmic vulture's singing suspended from opacity by sphinxes

your gullets continue to burn
that we know
as is a tangible raft of meteors
divided & removed from final motion as cause

in a more objective tenor
we see Haiti
'as a complex group of schists ...'
of 'extrusive' & 'intrusive' igneous rocks
of 'altered limestones' & 'shales'
& 'conglomerates' 'along the axis of the Cordillera Central' *

& 'the Haitian Massif du Nord' *
with the 'surface rocks'
& the 'Eocene limestones'
the both of you squirm
dashed against this backdrop
against your crimes sustained in motionless weariness

if we ask you
of 'Mesophytic vegetation'
of 'Haitian oaks'
of 'West Indian cedars'
you are useless

as to 'Cacti' & 'dwarfed thorn trees'
your threats have failed you

the 'avocados' & 'zapote'
the 'exotic' 'breadfruit' & 'guava'
can never suffice by synthetic approaches

by fevers from a God given chalice
we have accrued in the substance of your dipole
an 'overbearing forfeit'
a maledictive withering

so intensively gathered
that the winds you once provoked can no longer burn
or dismember in your favour

above the niveous dove & the vultures
we send as special harbinger
incarnadine crows

a telepathic heron
with gifts of Ytterbium
of Polonium
of sealess iodine spray
flying back & forth from our charismatic ferment
with dogmatic toil
& clairvoyant abasement

we who confer with the discipline of the cenobites
graphospastic with conviction
bloodless & intuitive with omen

we
the refined oblation
the precise double movement of rays
like a blistered sketch of citron
embroiled across blazing horizons

& in the less astral aspect
we are bones engaged in deadly lightning battles

because
we conceive the crows as camouflaged pleroma
the telepathic heron
as electric cemetery squalls

therefore
as a fitful moon in Rada voudou *
we've come to know the raging Petro endemic
as the black invisible sensate
& we proclaim as our kindling rainless solitary lava

in the cholera of its unclaimed connectives
flowing as blank rotational assembly

& here we must stress our harmolodia of goading *
our morose in-stellar lamentation

for we were snatched from our former existence
as absence & presence in a void of compound abrasions
drowning in murky cataracts & confusion
yet
our dauntless alabaster motives
ringing
in the beauty of Dahomean translucence
as Haitian lunar suns transpire
in lingering visual ignatics *

therefore
we must address your intensive fates
as excommunicated ciphers
we
with our enlarged auricular mayhem
with the combinatory fact of our nervous colouration
with our sudden Petro drumming symbolic of Erzulie *
Goddess of the whip
of bleeding
of barrage

'every muscle is tense'
'the knees are drawn up'
& the fists are clenched so tightly
that the nails 'draw blood from the palms'

in a trance which solemnly withers
therefore
we empower the points between 'androgeneity' & 'omniscience'
'phallic principle' & 'childbirth'
between 'farming' & leguminous 'fertility'

because of such electrokinetic
we've come to inhabit feluccas
greenish interior feluccas
to sail through transitional sequel as
floating to a higher ontology of waking
in a rain of scattered speculums
like darkened vapours & seedlings
as a bitter kind of caravel
summoned to a pitch
inside a new & verdurous nova

& as the archetypal optic
we have the character of explosive rivalling genes
spun from galactic tornadoes
as amplification & grafting
as in the one solar eye seen from the dark as sufficient
as seductive
as a de-explosive magnet
as a scintillating pulchritude
as a salt within an orthogonal ray

here
we've shattered
inoperable plain song
therefore

we speak with the same incessant elusives
with riddling poltergeist connectives
with the maturated scarring
with the ceaseless untenable bone grafts
blurred between albescence & crow

or bloody mangrove eaglets
feeding from special iodine waters
so as
to keep you both coupling
to keep you as harassed & famous pilgrims
turned
as weakened & fallen suns
around the gravity of vacuums

we keep you hounded by our hatchlings
with your obsessed & stricken blood counts
which they drain
spurred by the fire of all their liminal dismantlings
being embodiment as disjunctive potash

the incarnadine crows
we've mingled with our relics & our teeth
as they ferociously litter
your garments with a palpable strychnine

therefore you are marked
with tortured spellbinder's urine
with inverted ganglionics
with messages condemned through amphoras

yes
your souls combined & laced with sullage
with dense & intractable vevers which slither *
with sunless sea horse gangrene

& in this dazzling zone we call the jackal's furnace
we conduct through the birds
the essence of a fiery moral campaign
as an eclectic maze
at the water base of atoms

we
of old Dahomean breeding
with cosmic Petro scowling
leave you both in the act
in the frenzy of the loa's copulator's prism *
sniped
by flying Bardo crows
by ancient mercenary vultures
relentless
fumatory
fractious
scalding"

The Stratospheric Canticles

This book is dedicated to my parents
BIRDIE and WILL
both of whom have passed into the great perpendicular

The Mime Tornado

Whirling
in this burning circular aviary
in this greenish stellar intensity
greeting the fire of my own shadow
with its simultaneous spurs
erupting from linguistic ferret
from the black domesticity of arrogance like a wind
absorbed in solar reptile signals
I greet its invincible ire
in the penetrating flux of its harried angular journey

it is a syllabus of glass & of ants
roving
like a living mutational turquoise
a lamp
an aperture of vireos proto-nomads hurtling through rivers of
 [swirling lunar haemophilia
heated by blank Egyptian kindling moons
here I am on a raft
of instinctive gemstone tumbling
on a raft
of rainy black & red molten
calling on my shadow
with all the colour
emptied from its treasonous mime tornado
so that eternity ingests the force of blazing tourmaline infects

infects charged
with the stunning topology of ignition with the empty transmission
 [bodies taking on
the momentous characteristic of the transmute specific
unravelling the tourniquet of hydrogen as in the songs from bodiless
 [sun bells

the black sun levels
where karmic stains are transmogrify

& the thoughts
meridian
like the name of a cloud passing into anomalous writhing

my shadow
the occult
the tunic enclave
over-arched like a beacon minus its wretched cyclical entrapment
a beacon in a floating citron granary burning from its ubiquitous
orbiting fountain
from its ironic wellsprings of torment
Its oasis oif gases
incessant
mutagenic
heraldic
boiling

The Psychotropic Squalls

To peer into the obverse
into smoking cane field erratums
as if haunted with the steamy colitis of whirling iridium
cancellations

as in the saliva of newts
one sees the intestinal raging of deltas
of blackened sea giraffes osmotically split into simultaneous alums
above a judgemental sea glistening with Richters

like a weakened neutron egg
its fissioning petrol mirages like spirals of irregular hunting geese
flying through flames of ulcerated smoke & gargantua
hissing a blank imperial greenness
rising above dense jetties of cobras

the shocking demise of the sea
the unlivingness of its winds
scorched by irradiations of shaking brine incisions
the burning gulfs of sun with a glint of explosive Mandean utopias *
shocks against Old Testament linear prophetics
of Jeremiah
or Ezekiel
or the bony frozen finger shaking stunted alchemical missives
from a moon burned Judea
no more than a mechanically burning moat focused on smoky
spellbinder's disruptives
where the motion of the soul is delayed
reduced to flattened agnostic secular smoke
to a terrestrial rage which eliminates its sensuous heavenly fires
its stunning unreplicated angers
its sudden selenium spirals
its fire which staggers across the pseudo-faultlines of pre-replicated
    [judgement
its flirtation with spirits of enriched Draconian plankton

so that the soul with its amber of flashing microbe drachmas
with its wounded tourmaline divisibilities
flaming within a light of smeared tornado weathers
within a shower of black fish scales & spleen
is entombed
within a blank thirstless psycho-motion
falling from a furnace of stars
which both flares up and freezes
which inculcates a flawed microbial botany
as in hypnotic grammatical emulsions

within a hollowed elliptical opening where we witness old Egyptian
    [surgeries
where the dead magically rise up from mazes
& stare in a language of scorching totemic anomaly
spawned in heretical miniature
their phantoms
seeping from quadrilateral sutures
from brief

violent
renunciatory squalls

uprooted
armed with the weaponry of ghouls
& broken birch tree lizards
seasoned by the light of psychotropic angles
blazing in the middle of a green Venusian interior God
singing
as if
in the fumaroles of anguish
with an inclement bleeding
with a littered corona
of unstable altimeter reverses

The Mesmeric Remora

> A name given to fishes of the family *Echeneididae*
> They attach themselves to sharks, turtles and
> large fish, and are transported by them ...

"Living within this floating insula gold
this gleaming salted gold
ploughing through waves of blood
crossing the fumes of ghostly Navanax volcanos*
across steaming anthrax Barracuda
within the acoustic pharmacopoeia of sisal

flitting through a mirror of exploding analgetics
suffused with eerie verdurous rays
my gills
like eyelids
opening & closing by twilight
staring across extinguished gene lakes
my scales
runically glistening like alchemical nerve rings

The Stratospheric Canticles

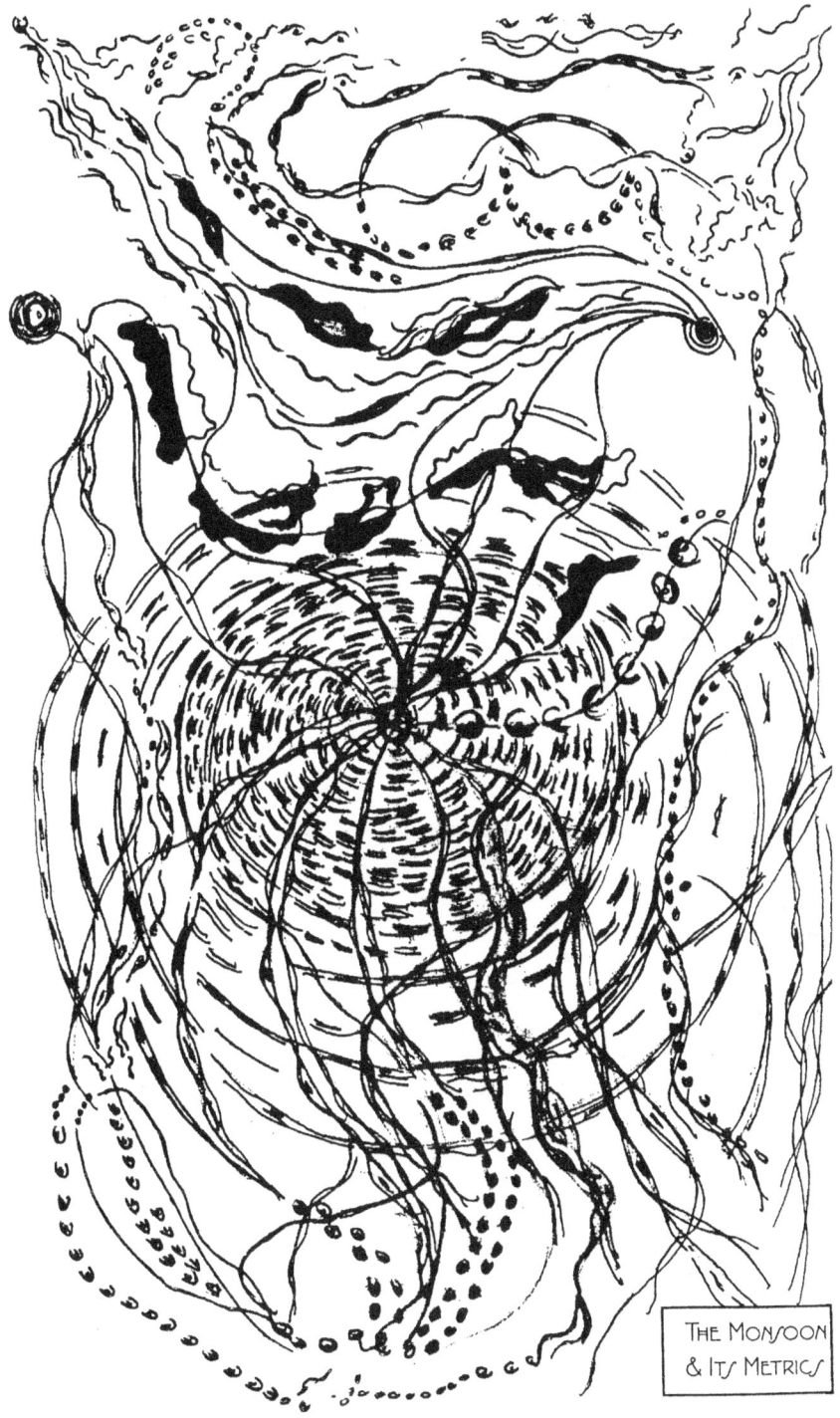

THE MONSOON & ITS METRICS

like a penetrant astral coral
claimed by a great density of scarabs

each measurement of sea
a spinning butane cartouche
in which I see myself
reflected in meandering parallel flesh
of the sharks' oracular missives

I am swarming in decibels
in chronicles of electric mirror suns
in telepathy by watery sonar grasses
growing from tumultuous neon rudiments
forming a transparent flank of whales
my pottage entwined
by transposed ocular burns
casting spells
with dreadful trespasser's foci

taking on a soundless liminal punishment
in order to endure eons
in order to infuse my eyes with smoking electrical banishment
attempting to scale my own gregarious anaemia

I wish to spawn
angelic germination
by means of blank pre-Cambrian raven
shedding my own time warp
my blighted osteological urines
by ceaseless admixture of terror

I am the ironic weeping fern
the fish with a bird in its discs
the animal subsumed by a voice"

Song in Barbarous Fumerole of the Japanese Crested Ibis

The wings pierce as if they were eternity.
— Shuzo Takiguchi

The Japanese Crested Ibis is now extinct.

"To claim as arcane vapour
ruination by intrigue
by kindled leprosy morays
so that I take up in my glottis
these moral hallucinogens which actively dim
which nourish themselves on behalf of active heavenly terror

as if forking my verbs with cryptography
with bird interrogation
with a haunted crystallography of deception
mentally cross-fertilized with defective aural lobotomies
so that I momentarily sing
with a cosmic catch in my wings

floating above
a black waterfall of rye
dazzled by partial torments
by seeming in-seminal scatterings
by snow in smoking germinal mazes

it could be said that my blood has been scorched
by intensive Venusian plasma
by updrafts of wheat
by molecules that slaughter
my throat continuously parched
by wild in-secular genetics
by unfiltered parchment
by incipient nerve cuisines
empowered by listless cranial singing
carving androgynous shapes with my voice

me
an ominous fluttering angel
kept aloft by diagrams
of smouldering electrical truth

as a tempestuous solar charisma
I can never speak in terms of oceanic remorse
or with the temperament of fictitious remedial doves

no
I am heightened by sudden sociological flaws
by prisms of seasoned parallel tornadoes

though shattered by various Saxon devices
I am the flame throughout the soaring absolute
I denigrate
I take on sanguine territorial opposition
with a force
enriched
with untoward fertility
with a dominate tendency to waver
with excessive a-regional metrics
with inhaled phantasmics
spilled on fortuitous migrational soils
there is ermine
there is discourse by nugget
there is scarification by increase

each of my echoes spinning through pictographic parabolas
graphic
with indecisive incest
which abstractly reduces
which plummets
into the frothing systemic of bees

a crepuscular arachnoidal utterance by sun bells
by pestilential archive
by vivid tourmaline exposure

there is expressed interstice
notational temperature by prophet
by sun exposed Greek

therefore,
a palace erected in bone plazas
to worship each grainy avian heaven
each tumultuous spire by detraction
so that there exists the one true clarity
the cloudy singular beam
more blinding than sun noons on Mercury

pinnacle by rot
by hovering phoneme & tremor
by sorcerous frigate & plasma
by flaming interior sign
by defenceless grenadine morals
as with Enoch *
I continue my metamorphosis
singing in capsized tarantula tree
melodramatic by despair
cogitation by a sense of entrapment
split along the cusp of a-tonal meridians

each guttural burst
struggling at great odds
at hieroglyphical knife point
dazed with magnetic electrical fuchsia

each of my wingbeats as death
as co-existent termination
as spoiled rudiment by colour

so I splice my lamentations
& open the diachronic

to spawned confusional rotations
amidst the equator of sundogs
heated by corrupted memorial sparks

my beak aligned with cryptographic cunning
with tantric scratches inside my steaming ink well treaties
my aggressions in tune
with an aching heraldic nopal
its coronal glare
flashing upon a-clinical watery mnemonics
filled with carnivorous morphine & diamonds

flying in Bardo *
above the scattered wrath of oneiric sesame pontoons
eclectic with my knowledge
of furious marginal germs & diseases
hyper-extended with discord
those bony schismatic ghosts
fused by synchronic retinal burning
drawing from the sky
a milk
seasoned with phlogiston & Hittite galvanics

yes
chandas flecked *
with sulphurous heretical clauses

because
I deny
& re-invigorate
I tear down
I re-pontificate
the bile from empty animal invasions

breaking through poisoned civil cataleptics
entangling quotidian farm worlds
with my traitorous acids

culled
from a barbarous daily wine

here I am
winged

The Stratospheric Canticles

with oracular sun-dust flowers
my eyes scattered into translated demon
like a blue demonic spy
sailing across transparent carrion planes
so as to re-inhabit the dead
so as to scan the weightless centigrade margins

in one simple respiration
I summon the tendencies of electrocuted corpses
the stony wrath
of drowned Phoenician sailors

my voice drills
with North Asian alewahs *
akin to compounded rock points on Vesta or Ceres

yes
I drain from stars pre-glottal alluviums
moth ceramics
a chalice of rote
pestles shaped
by incipient hulls of deadly carbon grams

I sing
across distracted ingress baying
with sounds
not even the dead can decipher

I can only increase funeric confusion
the invisible force which uplifts the void
which ingests the force of negation & mirage

yet I sculpt
in weakened anti-negation
spasms rampant with fire
distorting by quotidian thumb piano

by plagues which sustain gregarious verbal gestation
subsumed from susurrations extracted from the scattered

logistics of Titans
from the fevered optical beams
spilled from greenish sundial eternities

Ramses *
or Hatshepsut *
or Akhenaton *
invading as cherished cyclical spores
their luminescence by blankness
by swarming alchemical moons
by bewildering errata
as in rum by higher being
by serpentine
& flowing whiplash ideology

above all
I've cosmically transmuted the atmospheric bone
the dementia enveloped by protest
by turquoise weight
& somnific solar inclusion
singing by eclipse torrent
by waves of flame erupting from mirrors & dreams of post-extinction

a geneaology of circles
beyond aphids' scribbling
& logical strontium dialectic

my bleeding unbearable shadows
brewing

a sumptuous fever of poetic electrical charisma
its lightning shafts
of snow & rum & blood
mixed with the grains
of stunning axial omegas"

The Stratospheric Canticles

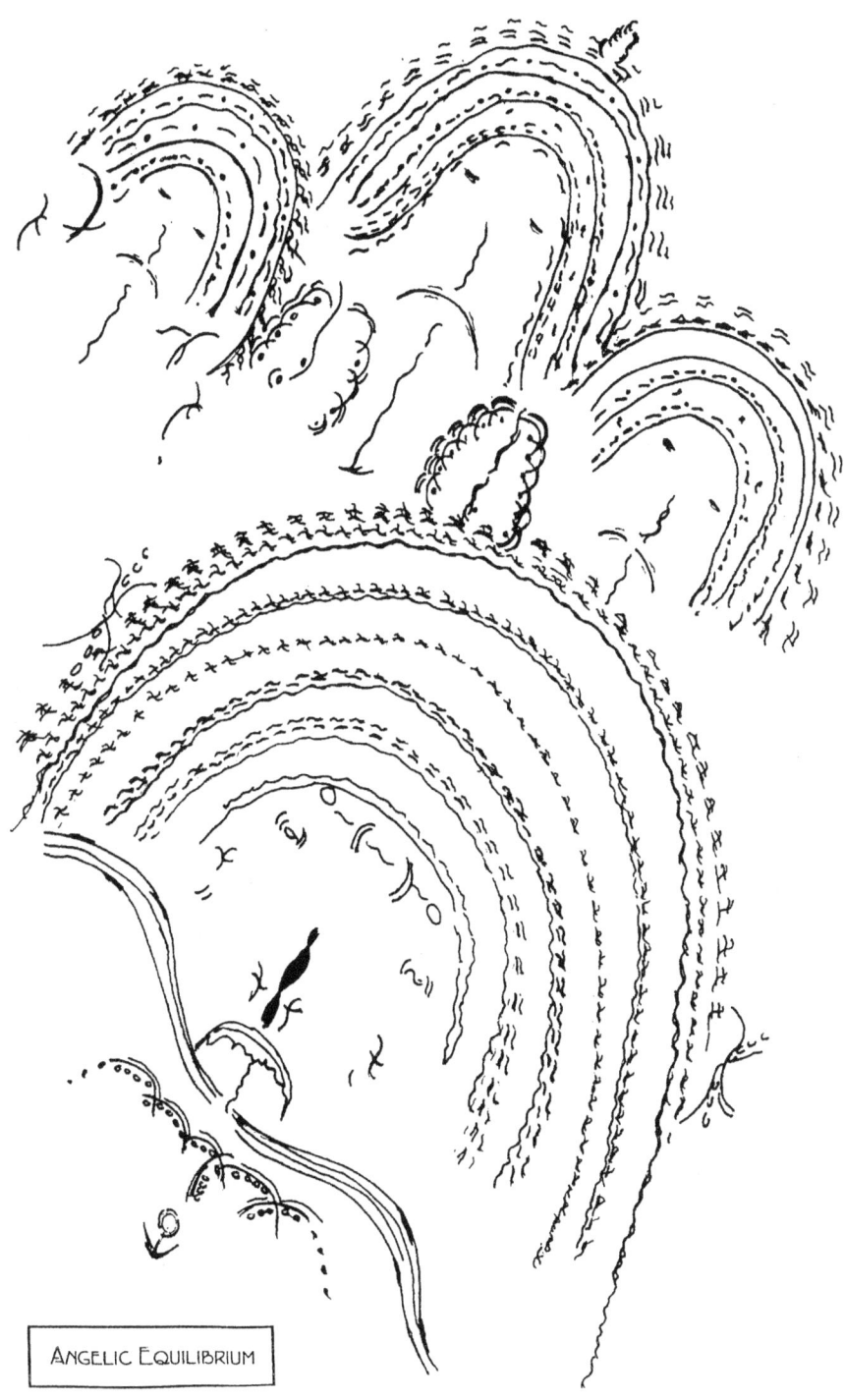

Angelic Equilibrium

Against the Temperature of Time & Corrosion

Living
beneath the murderous pressure
of time & corrosion
one is transfixed by glints
by a mirage
which fulminates diamonds
into a greenish albino blackness

which deflects the staggering
from Newtonian labour for bread
for earning ducats which burn
like illusional marionettes
miming a deadly archery to the veins

they sing falsely
like the intestinal coinage of time counters
who enunciate the rhetoric of worth
who tear the flame from one's inches
by means of blank quotidian ire
daily
counting one's head
like nervous leprosy wardens

lengthening
& shortening one's cudgel
so as to replicate imbalance
attempting to ensnare the bell in one's soul
by leaving the sun scrambled
by having the zodiac partially burned in one's fractional houses

in response
one becomes
fratricidal
hounding
tempestuous as a delta
with the ghosts of drowned cobras

one stores up insults
one takes on the face threatening neural volcanoes
one truly becomes severed
dreaming homicide by intransigence
by lightning burns
by flames from the black widows' love nest

the struggles
the vices
the work
the absolute hatred for dominance & capital
nurturing the blood
from the rum of one's woundings

lighting capsized tornadoes
with winged delusional edicts
pacing back & forth
like an explosion of dried cataracts

so that
the absent biology
the mirrors of rain & dust
erase
the terse mechanical dropsy of limits
& become the fierce axial exchanges
the murdered dove growers
who resurrect
a series of proto-ambulations
a movement of lime & melted vertigo
against horography
against Greco-Roman linear increases

yes
to take as one's body eclectic meridional winds
to extract from unknown seas a bevy of Incan compass reports

so if one says
wave after wave of concentrated snow fish
or if one says

a tonnage of raw selenium malice
one suddenly takes on a dense resurrectional rubidium myopia

yes
it is because
the moon is always capable of meandering modes & mathematics
of creatureless blood stains
of shattered pre-Socratic dice & upheaval

which absolves the self
of time games
& blood zones
which hallucinate & transpose their burdens
to an oblique terrace
where human & angel human
take from each of their ciphers
crystals
crossing points
confusions

each of their maniacal murmurs on a sun boat
across voidless athanasias
sailing through
medial stellar rarefactions
so that each
of the bodies one possesses
will exercise its fabulous exercise pestles
its acrobatics of exile
its high collusional dialectics
rising
like the highest craters
amongst the 9 known planets

one then surmounts
the flaming strychnine concentrations
gambling away one's salacious personal frauds
so that one floats by suspension
imbibing the force
of interminate comets & hail

Apprenticeship

> ... between impulses and repentances,
> between advances and retreats.
> — OCTAVIO PAZ, *Eagle or Sun?*

Here I am
posing in a mirror of scratch paper sonnets
sonnets as rare
as a live Aegean rhino

absorbing the cracklings of my craft
its riverine volcanoes
its spectacular lightning peninsulas
emitting plentiful creosote phantoms
from an ironic blizzard of unsettled pleromas

scouring through years of unrecognized pablums
of constant arch-rivalry with extinction
bringing up skulls of intensive discourse
by the claws in one's mind
which seem to burn with systemic reduction

one then suffers poetic scorching by debris
by inaugural timber which flashes
by friction which flares up & harries
by unrecognized moltens collapsing in glass
of initial intuitive neglect

as if one's fangs
were fatally stifled by incipience
by verbal range war didactics
by territorial driftwood
by sudden undemonstrative detractions
awed
by the diverse infernos of Trakl & Dante
one's youngish body stands
devoured by reverential print trails
momentarily cancelled

by the loss of blasphemous nerves & upheaval
stung
by demeaning neutralities
ravaged
by a blank Sumatran solar psychosis
by a tasteless collision of rums in transition
by a conspiracy of obscured fertility by hubris

as one sucks in doubt from a wave of tumbling blister trees
there exists irradiations flecked with a gambled synecdoche
with indeterminate earthenware splinters
taking up
from aboriginal density
a forge of Sumerian verbal signs
cooked with a tendency
towards starfish hypnosis
towards psychic confrontational drainage
conducting one's frictions in a torrential furnace of osmosis & ire

yes
apprenticeship
means poetry scrawled in unremitting leper's mosaic
cringed in smoky interior cubicles
releasing various deliriums
as if pointed under a blackened Oedipal star
with its dark incapable tints
with its musical ruse of unspoken belladonna

poetics
an imaginal flash of Russian chamber lilies
stretching under a blue marsupial sun
like kaleidoscopic tumbleweed
fugaciously transfixed
upon an anomalous totem of glints
upon rainy Buenos Aires transfusions
above the urinal coppers of a flaming polar star rise

of course
kinetic

like magical malachite rivers
flowing from moons
blowing through the ¾ summits of motionless anginas

I've looked
for only the tonalities that scorch
which bring to my lips wave after wave
of sensitivity by virulence

yes
a merciless bitterness
brewed by a blue-black tornado of verbs
in a surge of flashing scorpion chatter
in a dessicated storm of inferential parallels & voltage
like a scattered igneous wind
co-terminus with the bleeding hiatus & the resumption of breath

resolved by flash point edicts
by consumptive stellar limes
by curvature in tense, proto-Bretonian fatigue

mixing magnets
juggling centripetal anti-podes & infinities
cracking the smoke of pure rupestral magentas

yes
hatcheries
floating through acetylene corruption of practiced mental restraint
to splendiferous vistas mingled with inspirational roulette
its mysteriums
always leaping like a grainy rash of scorching tarantellas
or leaking moon spun alloestophas *
as if speaking
in irregular glossological green Dutch

a frenetic seminar on febricity
a reiteration of hendecasyllabic agitation & stinging
a ferocious vacillation
explosive as random "aggregational" nodes

mimed by a black consonantal dissection
its maximal priority
forked at "hypotactic inclusion"
with isochronous internal procedure
with ratios
with phonic penetralia by distortion
primed by anomalous "nuclear accent"
by a cadence composing syllables & compounds

yes
poetics
its force
jettisoned by "hypotaxis"
by ... paratactic co-ordination
& fire

Explosive Decibel Journeys

>For Javier García Sánchez
>Author of *Lady of the South Wind*, whose
>central character commits suicide by explosion

Inside the catalytic mine field
there exists
the fire of antinomous poppies
the writhing of broken insect nodules
marshes limned with collapsing nitrate teeth
in an atmosphere
of kerosene & iceberg volcanoes

I am thinking
of dark obsessional blood edicts
of grainy migratory suns
spinning around a series of gloomy aqua tornadoes

spawned with the telepathy of ice bears
afire with fur & ancient Dionysian characteristic

with the blank specifics of a roaming cohesion
roaring
with an electrocuted mockery
into a bleak condensation of cobalt
flung into a dawn of broken intestinal ringlets

this dawn
explosively slanted with a fiery nautical intransigence
with blanched
stormy
meridian meteoritics
as if its smoke were Roman
bleeding
upright
contradicting
its anti-torsional eruptions
its sudden bloated carnivorous potentia
its protracted carnage by indifference
floating through rainy indigo explosions
floating through a palladium of "mineral ash" & anthracite & fervour

a stoking pressure
of stone
& coke
& fabric
with an intensity linked to pulmonary punishment
negatively slurring all the bodies of zinc

the weather of Leeds & Sri Lanka petrified
by "hygroscopic acid"
by gassy ambiguous rain attack
by the in-vital foods of negative in-vitality
the whole world
an ozone of wicked calendrical debacle
an insidious metallurgical illness
revolving through haunted strontium mazes
weakened as a dysfunctional eclipse furnace

terra firma
becoming a dark enfeebled nightmare relic
asked to take on the weight
of unnatural suckling fevers
the grain spores screaming facing scarification by extinction
the mine field ruthless with inverted skeletal waters
pumping up scars
so that the rock fish swelter with wicked selenium error

because
there exists
acidic complications
fierce animal anomalies
hatched by a terror of blackened firing powders
so as to face an intermittent breeding
a smoky lattice work of angels
blinded by spectral anginas
set against the life force
with the rusty simultaneous core of statistics
always under the light of merismatic smoke
of merismatic compromise
in the mine field
in the wicked hydrogen ekstasis
no longer combined
with the smoke of simple Iroquois signals
alive with the truth of Indian burial law

I am speaking of clouded Euro-centric sulphur
of the Javier García Sánchez creation committing suicide by explosive
timed against
the aboriginal magnets
against the utopian sun angles
miming flightless strychnine ravens
ignited by great diagrams of blood
as if explosions were a song
of instinctive deflagrations
of degenerate human sparks
poised upon a shaky "nitrocellulose"

or translations from a synonymous kind of cyclonite
spreading throughout the plane
affecting
the power of waterfalls
the Gersoppa *
the Kalambo *
the Middle Cascade *

yes
the Caspian Sea
the Peace *
the Don *
the Snake *
waters prognostically poisoned
in this smoky litmus corral

a spiral of agony
illumined
by "Wood meal" *
by "Aluminium powder" *
by "Dynobel" *
"characteristics
of permissible explosives"

yes
dichotomies etched
like a sullen bread
of parched elliptical powders

blowing apart the earth
like a naked fish on an altar

a disastrous Nobelian hymnal
brazen
with purely creosote tectonics
like a ghost suddenly spiralling off to sea
with savage earthquake metrics
like flash points
with the treacherous teeth of elongated nightmare tigers

of course
an insatiable sea roaring
beneath a sun of territorial cancellations
as if suddenly shifted moons
had taken on the weight of perpetual solar expansions
like an exploded mist climbing Antarctic willows

in the end
an illusional jasmine furnace
in which doves are smelted
in which fingers
are detached & reborn
between a terrified calendrics
& the eerie decibels of an insolvent limbo

The Stratospheric Canticles

> Not sun, not moon, not stars
> not the sudden green
> of lightning,
> not the air. Only mist.
> — RAFAEL ALBERTI

To paint
is to make a mark of mirrors
of genuine graphite slabs
poisoned
with mescal & olives

& each of their scorching medial colours
evincing the glow
of purple turpentine sierras
shadowed with a shaft of blue tubercular lightning
so that stones fly up like falcons
bursting in asteroidal twilight

The Stratospheric Canticles

THE SUBCONSCIOUS EYE

an aerial canvas
marked by transparent ocular ravines
with its "Intense colour"
its "agitated lines"
its "pessimistic convictions"
mined from smoking quinine soils

a gulf of fiery alpine cinders
like "calligraphic" scarlets
rising from smoky virginal hells
colliding with altimeter chartreuse
as an enriched traumatic grammar of squalls
a grammar
as in Matta
with his occulted balance of streaks
his fleeting micrometer aloes
his rays of precise acoustical jade
his juggled intensities
by inward explosion of fraction
by a trance of ungovernable burnings
as in a beautiful wind blown drought

sacrifice of still life by argumentative still life
so that there is motion
the retroflexion of orange & radical selenium fevers
into razored
"Prussian Green" glints
as in a ravenous wall of ivy
bursting with flameless medicinal dawns

a cataract of palaces
a-top the raging light of a-positional isotopes
sending out
a cherished collusional ray
across a series of trans-axial nerve fields

a flight of levitational acidics
fiery illusional rains
upon transfixed ruins of spectrographic novae

as in subconscious germinal neutralities
as in linguistic anopsia
equiponderate
with blinding chromosomal orchids
formed
in a precious breech of flotational cadmium
there exist rays
seen from the glass of glowing lava & brambles
existing as an image of working illuminant dragons
or the desiccated face of a crimson Assyrian singing demon
shining through a luminous bio-chemical cosmogony
with the gift of miraculous terror
with exotic Byzantine plumage
gleaming by formula
by the secret flow of metamorphosis
like crackling "inductors" spewing cosmogonic turquoise
statuesque osmium
whipping Saturnian electrodes

winds
yellowed
active
blowing by ionic motive
by doves & momentary glycerin fish circling
a fissure of glass
of miles & miles of vertical x-ray helium
like reddish invisible eruptions
fugacious
as with blue absorption lines
with their flairs
of autumnal deluge
with their carmine sigils
with their stormy climacteric phantoms
taking on the murky force of bi-pedal lagoons
within a shifting circumstance of cerulean
within the uplifted cholera
mixed with rotations of a heavenly halcyon sun
emitting its fires
into atmospheric volume

into blank reverential mutilation
so that the violet
the ochre
the chromium
the green
into fulminate Chinese Sienna
which is correlation by goddess
by blood creeping from the sorcerous heat of ambiguous
shellfish enclaves
enriching the rose of prolific cortical timbers

paint
able to conjure
"Cyanine Green" floods
flotational cobalt moons
hallucinated umber
like a chrysalis evolved
from dying charcoal fish
resurrected by leopards
swimming the rims of judgemental Armageddons
divining the leaping fires from a raging blood snapper furnace
its fabulous fumaroles of anguish
its fugitive uncharted scarlets
like a cunning seminal beast
a palpable beast
ensnared
"in winding arcs from a central core"

like an epic
simultaneous in its range
violent
expressive
psychic
full of whiplash
& toxic sepia coils
like microscopic emulsions
climbing a rotted insistence
more concrete
than the spoiled invasions of a-ravenous trilobites

again
dense visual grammar
discontinuous indigo
as a charismatic optical mirage
so that one can insist that the life force be magenta
hewn by the crepuscular hubris of syllogistic monsoon
by error which burns
in a strange family of grafts
which meanders across chromas
soaked
in a flash of flooded wordings
in language of old volcanic harassment

in the convulsive exclamations
of the erupting Aconcagua *
or Cotopaxi in Ecuador *
or Karisimbi in the Congo *
or heated West Irian flowers
hissing and hissing again
in Javanese volcanic reflex

one cannot speak of albino reindeer mountains
or of acceptable cogitations on the history of Mt. Blanc
instead
one tends to travel by surbation
across explosive scorpion beds
across indefinite orismologies
as if painting
with tensely riddled verbal scaupers
opening the beauty with dysphoric protean realias

then one hotly flees ideological panopticons
therefore
the being is bodiless
ascending
panoramic
pure
above the green ventricles "of the brain"
one becomes largifical

livid
able to impatronize randomy
singing in Assyrian madrigal & whisper
in shapes which defy
the plausibilities of sound
the measurements
the impackments
the calendars of old flesh embedded in tables of terror

therefore one ingests
imparisyllabic suns

so as to burn up psychic circumscription by implosion
so as to parallel & magically engulf the power sustained in cyclographs
so as to negate bleak hatcheries of dogma
so as to provoke the hereditary flight of disembodied vipers

to leave
a fractionalized circumference
akin to the rising glimpse of Heteroousian nightmares
to leave
negated orthotropic osteological hollows
so as to fuse with unicorn & osprey minerals

an otic penetration
achieved by singing in sordino
in tense soritical optics
in a living pendulum of sweltering sotto voce

as in Spain
with its splendiferous motifs of aroma
with its lemons
with its jets "of strong pepper"
with its Moorish sibylline Granadas
with its Strange "Berberesque" Andalusias
with its tumultuous instinct for scholarship
its astral geometries
its runic struggles against the weight of "phantoms"

as in El Greco
with his "despotic fantasy" of "elevation"
his "silvery pallors"
"pale yellows"
"green lights"
rising
through supra-conscious archives
spinning around the poles
of "miraculous paradox" & infinity
one thinks
of the stormy "View of Toledo"
with its enriched perpendicular darkness
with its power to stammer & transfix
with its heavenly optical thirst

what concerns one
are the mixings
the saturations
seeping across virgin crepuscular glass

yes
rovings
as in the metrifications of various movements of silk
one thinks
of "sand"
of "fire"
of "extinction"
of "Late Devonian glass sponges"
of "calcareous algae"
formerly teeming in the "Paleozoic"
genetics
cast without warning into the nucleic fire pit
into sudden arithmetical negatives

one thinks of human genes adrift
the former cornucopia of Europe
dazed
by self-inflicted malevolence
by a ratio of powerless in-breeding

of chaotic in-diversity
so that the ghosts of the Berbers re-emerge in Iceland
taking over the North
as various figments of tribulation

by life from Berber seed
there is ascent
from walled-in munitions law
from compost evolved from neon-plutonium sewage
from the niggling betrayal of doves & their grains
one then is extracted
from plutonic primary odours
from various burning abysses
the empire of ices transmuted
beyond the Roman rational brain

no more
the dire threat from cartographical blackness
from the cold alluvial fires which threaten with strontium
whose errors are threaded with a tensely riddled stasis

the linear world
& its shattered inversions
its meandering colonial nerve ray
fractured
clinging to mistreated diasporas
attempting to fine tune its current
after its voltage has withered
as if its praxis remained convinced
in post-mortem deracination

its remnants dazzled by rampaging scorpions
across genetic collapse
of its Saxon storage house

one can now celebrate
its first anniversary in nothingness
its ultramarine annihilation

the non-white cogito as fugitive
dressed up in splendiferous day moss
in Manganese & Viridian oyster with Emerald

an intrusive succubus edict
speaking in plaintive mongoose structure
rhyming in sonorous tornado iguana

in protean advancement
one takes up linguistic spillage
drowning
& re-ascending from tides of molten
like the force of a snake which scales
a steaming tree of riddles

scaling
like a deeply infected sigil
in order to compose its own plenitude
in order to magnify by hypnotic darkness

its impressionistic trance
at the osmotic centre of vibrational corollas
with the ironic stare of a dark anathema prophet
expounding upon
a luminous body of cataracts & pillage
a bluish body
erected upon primeval cyanosis

because
verbs pour in a torrent of intense fertility
like a cycadaceous fuel
wrathful
like a force of nerves brought to the fore by medicinal plankton
wild
as in a language of exploded espaliers
a heated hectographic aesthetic
by which
one multiplies one's person
by the power of ravenous hebetics

yes
a verbal rate pulsing from a golden heliogram
eating into the very nerves of reptilic ascension
into the scorched triangle of havoc
so that the lotus
with its Egyptian mummification by both grain & by star
is equal to the asteroidal ranges of Ceres

yes
to poetically render
to paint
is to dissolve a fleece of frankincense & diamonds
with a temperature which reddens into eclectic willows of jade

in its primeval grain
thought is exceptional abscission
from a tense Kantian enclave of contingent skeletal rays
from an abyss which logically mentates
from the seismic flaws of a conditioned surgical sun
maimed with conditional finalities
its out-put
taut
with in-circular greys
with a sickened grenadine pallor
circling the void
like a staggered eclipse model
its philosophical mephitics
Neptunian
in the derangement of its tumultuous aphotics

this sun
the splinters of the Occidental mental clause
Spun in the soul
like an even sum of strychnine
so that one is only capable of egregious multiple stuntings
which dismember the mind
when facing incalculable noumenas
the cleansed Moroccan blood in trance
flowing throughout the tendrils of trance

therefore one denounces
physiology by classification
by simulated stratagem
by heightened rotational contingency pattern
by alms
forcefully compelled
to honour figments & alterations by disastrous material confinement

one needs
the mind unloosed by wavering
by groping
in & out of its own liminal hamlets
darting throughout the presence of shaking marginal Calliopes
like an indefinite solstice
based upon greenish herbiferous cremations

a zodiac which spins
in the service of creatureless chaotics
Olympian
in its seismic electrical content
its waves
its generating impact
by opposition & force
& force by counter-force

one must palpably contend
that life eternally erupts
from the flow of the absolute
that contingency is an item
a stare
a hallucination
which draws in
which burdens
a false incestuous liberty cooking its parables with tin
with demarcations
which rivet
which anaesthetize the rituals in one's implicit orgone energy
those lateral harmonics

those denouements which erupt at the pinnacle of one's bodily actions
as with the sudden flight of Dobu shamans
or like "North Borneo" seance rowing in the "Boat of the Dead"

this is the spoken word of high nomadic soils
the exquisite interior of levitational lilies & winds
alive with phonetic rapture
with their ritual Mercator publics
their hieratic ceremonial spoilage
flitting around omens
fused with a haunted Uranian topology
a Uranian indigo & phosphorous
possessed
of the nervous condition of ghosts
emitting with each breath
stunning oracular leanings
so that one speaks
of marginal dialectics
of traitorous bursts of flame
of possessive claustrophobia

yes
illumination by biographical exile
luminosity by spiral
by awakened burning tangles
so that the aura intuitively irradiates
intensity by suspicion
by a flash of sullen nutations

at times
one takes on lightning by gram
as if haloed by circling glycerin nuggets

one's eyes
more than hurtling candle power
more than the force of syllogistic arcanums

so therefore
one takes within one's heart

the elliptical shining of galaxies in winter
become snow
become aged intestinal ringlets
become a pathological logos of radii
stammering
with dissonant gull marks
with an unstable virus instared by patterns of heat

the limitations which inhibit
the phantasmata which obscure
can only sing in weakened Kirilian denial
in fortuitous solemnity
yet
remaining organically weightless
tested
by tenacious cosmic squalls
by a tragic array of suns destroyed at the swirling peak of charisma
by dioramas which levitate by internecine dementia
so that being is denied the source of longevity
the axial strife of harmonics
which lengthens & refines the fire of heavenly grammars
which accumulates parsecs of thirst
which inspires Uranian mutational topologies
into a fiery altimeter of forks & rays

because
to leap through the spirit of burning
one must exorcise disaster
one must transmogrify its infernal nuclear crevasses
one must possess stamina

then the fire of the automatic organs
then the "radial velocity" at the "centre" of one's "Mass"
strengthening & spawning a scintilla of riches
a superior organicity of lightning waters
at play in a curious Lepton circus *
in a potent flask of sonar utopias
sending signals
across barriers of pent-up micrometer damage

into the "Imago Ignota" *
into the quizzical foundations of arcane

it can be said that one is unified by pressure
by an intensity which mingles in sub-bodies of radium
crossing & re-crossing the endless enclaves of heaven

the Milky Way
a single territorial nuance
a single brush with totality

& one exists
as no more than a living moth
as no more than a shelter with biometric extension
announcing in bluish crystal order
the delimited magnitudes
of Proxima Centauri *
of Procyon *
of Sirius *
of Groombridge *
of the lesser stellar lilies of Eridanus *
of the sudden flight of our earthly minimal sun

& this minimal sun
with its aura of heated bituminous etchings
with its flotilla of carbon wafting into our biliously seasoned
optic canals
into our sighted ozone mazes
so that
there is nourishment from its core
from its ionic orgone rains

a lean terminal brilliance
which sears
which electrifies
with its spinning carbonic gases
gases
by no means mechanical
glazed as they are
by a din of humming brush work angels

by a series of angels
flying through deafening embrasures

angels
who conduct themselves across gulfs
angels
at the spectacular gates of a flaming Heliopolis
angels
who carry Andromedan fragments away
to the 8 minute distance of the sun

then there is the blackened Hebrew aspect
like a cloudy dictator's broach
with its animal rays faltering from a defective beryllium zone
this monarch
hovering in a stupor of dread
within the shadow of powerful moonless soils
nevertheless
leaving a filter of discourse
at the fount of alien conundrums

here one speaks of inferior angels
angels endowed
with superior termination
collectively contoured to matter
more than photographic interferometry
less than telepathic medial Sufis
these angels
conducting the flight of the soul
across a darkened somatological gravity

across a music of enchained harmolodiums
flying by means of leaky transitional polemic
turning back on themselves
like a flock of diurnal Greek logicians
maintaining a vulgus balance
on a crumbling faultline of grams
their energies
carving small glottics into a rutless carrion treatise

one reflects upon Democritus
who is only compelled
by the stinging of bodies
by "divisibility" & leakage
transfixed by the "void in compound bodies"

the thought of the West
spawned from these laborious bewitchments
these negative cornucopias of grief
focused on the viperous element of rational centrality
on the mimed physiology as pinnacle

thought condensed within the principality of fraud
always embraced by blockages & plague
& the model for genius
poised upon fractional maiming

"Kant argues"
for the void of "necessary being"
for the elaborate quality of separation
for the critical kinetics of reasoned imperative
so that he blisters the intellect with his gaze
with his weighted copious treatise
with its stony symmetrical nerve

argument by droplets of seasoned mercury
lined up
in the irritating stamina of line

one must live for the exploded seminal burden
for the lack of afflicted contingency & weight
for the anti-clepsydra of air

therefore one speaks
not from abstract oppositional marrow
but from the level of the greenish tourmaline pole
connecting earthly stratums
with verdurous astral suns
burning above interjacent animal empyreans

the wheat of anomalous vultures & doves
piercing motionless pyretic tornadoes
with weightless oratorios of light
unlike the dotted line
the discontinuous errata
twisting in the muscular deaths of the plague
where the mind
in old dimensional bone
locks its clouds into dangerous skeletal ceramics
into a minimal cervical pre-history
into no more than a fierce dialectical nettling
where bodies erode
into a brutish amalgam of fragments
into metropolitan surgical pontoons
polluted
by occidental solar dioxide
stupified
by a-luminant gusts of remorse & confusion
like a blithe invidious falconry
crippled
by a stormy distillation of genes
frozen
in the humid drafts of the Jurassic
the wings of the birds
flailing at imparted boundaries
like dusty grafts mired in naked quantification

then one indeed is distracted by catastrophe
by the great black hidrotic fire
fissioning
straining above angular hierologies
toward the luminous blackness
of the "Northern" oriental caudex
toward the pole of Sohravardi *
toward the black light of Najm Kobra *
where one explores the enriched photinos
of a stupendous supersensory oasis
the ocular flash of stratospheric canticles
hovering in the mist

of the "crepusculum vespertinum" & the "crepusculum matutinum"
neither day nor night
nor night nor day
an intense flotational blazing
wafting into the "Emerald Rock" of "Hermes" *
into the metals which burst the bounds of the zodiac
into the realm of tempestuous jugular theophanies
into the life of rotational Shangri-La's
humming in revelatory ichthyosaur

a furnace of celebratory somniloquence
a furnace alive in unmeasurable fumarole
rattling the cartographical limits
speaking in paronomasia
in replication by reversible raven
parallel & flameless to angelic updraft
explosively flying
into the force of a-terrestrial compounds
so that its wings are metered & palpable by lightning
by insidious germinal plane
within a monitored anthropology
in a sky
mechanically fogged with congestion

each signal it gives
littered with expansive sclerosis
with chronicles of human killing fauna
history no more than an infected thermogenesis
no more than penultimate with raving & extinction

then the scientist with studied tarantula droplets
with his viperous molecular gaze
structures extraction
mines the gulf of the dead for genetics
with instructions tuned to the pitch of poisoned mania
so as to turn around in a sieve
explanations
neutered with murder & lying
so as to kill off the tropics

The Stratospheric Canticles

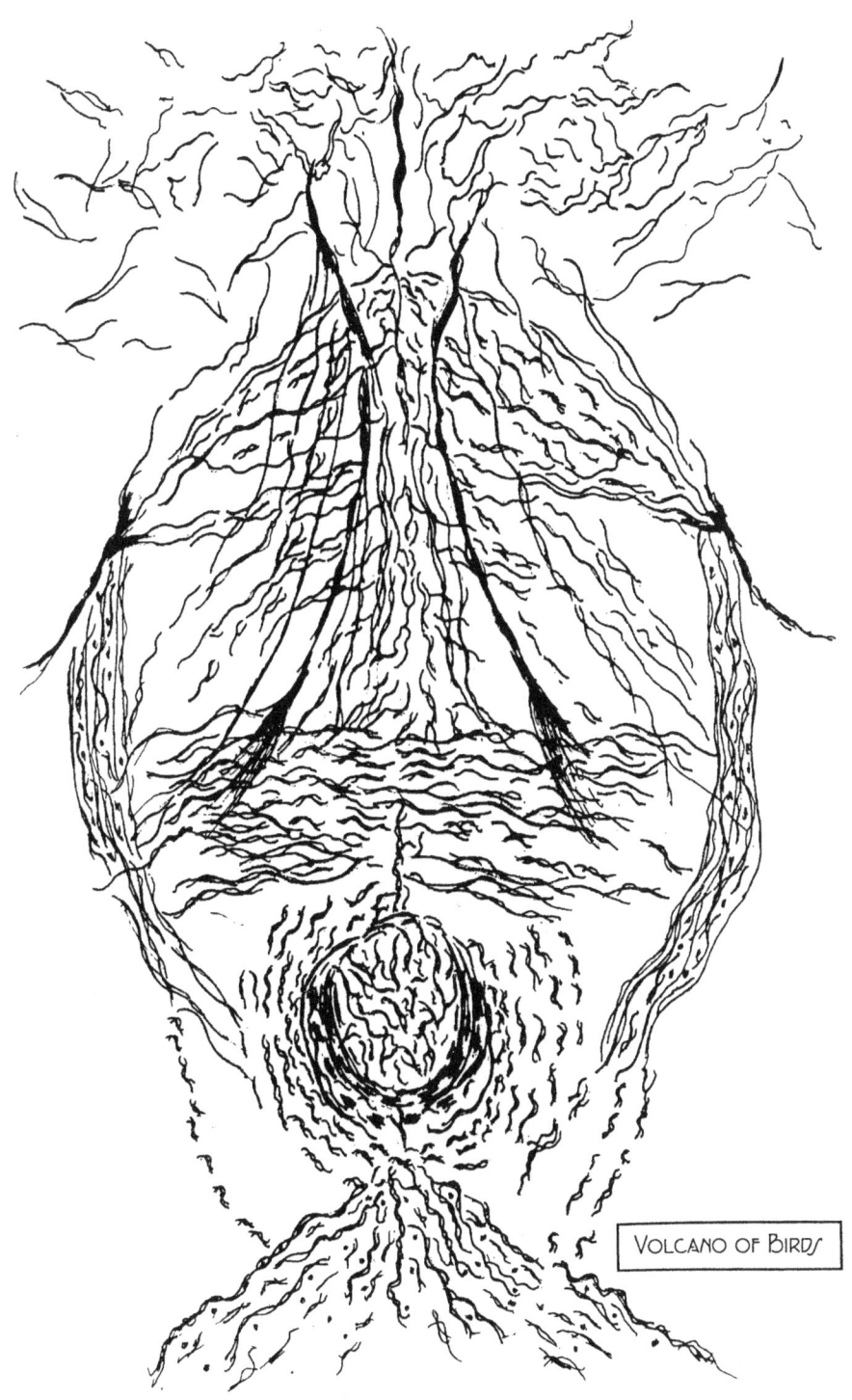

VOLCANO OF BIRDS

& make war on coronas
standing up
with beads on his face
as if sweating from the power of strong findings

this is not life
not the combinatory power of weeping torsos
swirling around a chart of cancelled lepton lagoons

one must angle one's amniotic juices from angered geranium blood
from a ferocious paramecium's bubonics
so as to faithfully transcribe
the tense cancellation of species
the Galapagos Hawk *
the Japanese Crested Ibis *
the Arabian Ostrich *
the Barbary Stag *
the New Zealand Bush Wren *
the Key Largo Wood Rat *
forced upon the pyre of clinical burning connectives

the wicked Euro-abscess model
claiming Democracy & engagement
claiming a factotum of decimals
eclipsing from life the fervour of condors
the ingestion of caimans
the savage sororicide of bears
so as to mechanically stoke the technicality of polls
to wash the terror of flesh from the general tax payer's grist

in its graph
it seeks the chemistry of vices
the forceful implanting of whispers
the gastric juices of bone
its pedestrian understanding
neutered by rot
by ingenious craving for negatives

so a being in Kansas
can dualistically rumble

with a spur in its sides
with a painful hook in its teeth
like toneless flesh
in a trampled sucrose experiment

awkward material conclusions
with meteoritic timing corrosion
with calculation by frozen micro-urn
with attempted equation of cold metallic termination
with the eyes of sealed off stellar snows
neutrino graphics concerned with rhetoric as seizure
as rotted clockwork panic
which evolves
into the working force of corpses
into tainted industrial obsequies

now eras reduced into digestible graphs
into the absence of feeling
so that one can measure the dead by labour

by a quantity of skulls
as if all the ashen memorials could live
as insomnious shop keepers' tonic
reseeded with zeal
but in reality co-terminous with the trilobites' extinction
akin to the bizarre schematics of the dredging up of ghosts
so that demons can be incessantly quantified
& projected on burdensome glass
by reasoned conceptual posing

their dastardly acts
resurrected
& transposed
into a vile jug of spiders
or a cataclysmic symposium of centipedes
their voices mixed with the sullen ethers of the drowned
which perpetuates decibels
where there is less & less a fire of falling axial mist
where there is less & less the odour of a strident jasmine prophet

Kaleidoscopic Omniscience

less & less a cleansed tourniquet of murmurs craving hieroglyphs &
borderlines of immortality through flying
by necessity
one is inspired to leap the tensors of the graph
& open up a hatch of heavenly aqua-marine
those foundries wakened from ingress digression
moving toward
Asian camouflage eternities
viridian sunbeam circles a
alive with onyx & climbing "Bengal Rose"

one sunders the stereotypic
which monitors
which closes in the fiery hamstring eagles

one must conduct one's electrics
as though in-bred by Gods
soaking from solar winds
power through explosive "Mimosa"

then one paints in the mind
an orange green & red Rothko
or Soutine's swirling hillocks at Ceret
or the flash point scarlets of Nolde

then one envisions flames in Islamic abstraction
intense Saturnian dawns
like a storm of solipsistic nitrate candles
fused in spinning auroral yellows
beneath a black unending heaven

then one intuits the raw inner number of Pluto
its psychic flailing through the Oort clouds *
& the sparse beginning of parsecs

now one glares at the unbeastly numbers
at the dazzling effects of this seeming nightmare idiom
at the seasonless distance which both stupifies & scalds

The Stratospheric Canticles

which eats up climacterics
& places the eye on a plane of smoky uredos

a summa of faceless lightning
across neb ulotic firmaments
across photo-genic concentrations
like suspended pitch
evolved from the ethers of revolving proto-galaxies

& their irregular condensations
like dramas of cataclysmic absorption Hydras
incessant Kelvin Richters
forming an invisible cave of prophetic neutron arrows
pointing to an era of emptiness
to a rich cognizance of terror
flying from the diamond gulfs of erupting indigo spectrums

one imagines momentum
as a giant Gargantua dove
invisibly eglantine
like a sonorous bleeding tree
blending its spores
with waftings across an endless germinal brilliance
like a fabulous cellular deepening
into a mirror with blackened igneous marks
fermenting transparent neutron fruit
such as the Fornax system *
the Draco complex *
the Andromedan wave *
like magnets of intense rotational mirage

this local radical world
at tangible flash point distance
at constant tangential remove
alive with dwarf elliptical motion
with its prairie of celestial objects on fire

so that one eats up ethane
with drift

with the tense psoriasis of character
as if each of one's bodily rooms had emptied their suns into the void
& become a blue circadian treatise magically swelled with eternity
then one forgets what death was like
its intermediate frenzy
its howling jugular waters
its large debacle of circles
its lighter & darker spasmodics
its ominous flight of disjunctive agraphia

one can no longer condense its force as a golden remedial hurdle
or as a genuine & necessitous punishment

one must live with the altimeter
with an eerie alchemical endlessness
which engenders a hypnotic parallel breathing
a breathing further & further removed
from an immense inconclusive bondage
from the limits of muscle & corrosive calf imprints

then one explodes
the insidious biological standoff with death

the groping
the muscular discontent
the rabies of standing alone in a powerful updraft of blankness

short of this
there is theology & rhetoric by phasma
attempting
to extract from these abstracts
enclosed chronological summas
a heavenly condition by duality

limited aerial lobotomies
etching terrestrial calamity
level by obscured level
in the interests of a European entropy

the proselytized printings of the word of life & death
the illusional advantage of monsters
trained to assault the believers
to taint them with false messages of fact

this is the light of daily Christian teaching
upon the Taino
upon the Iroquois
upon the Inca
the traducement & vilification
of the wooden fetish of the Yaka *
of the geometric leathers inscribed by the Fulani *
of the beaded blue calabashes as found in the Cameroon
the buzzing tones produced from the "Congolese nauga" *
derided as missing
as locked away in an opaque imperial curiosity

but art
evolved from charged impersonal regions
glistens
with the life of collective deadliness
so that all motions shine
in the quickened wind of higher music

a level removed
from the Renaissance ideal of the "sensitive outer ego"
of the negation of "constant essence"
when one absorbs the colours of Giotto or Botticelli

works summoned
by technically skilled guile
by the brazen execution of society in neurosis

to paint
is less & less from the colours of this earth
from its seeming cartographical borders
imposed by personality as barracuda
as the stance of a name with an obscure vivacity
its celebrity gathered

by vividly drawn gustatory habits
by wayward & labyrinthine mating procedure

there exist on other planes
the explosive Asiatic specific
"the portrait which is not in colours"
the depiction which fulminates at the pinnacle of interior axes

it is to paint
from the sources of black legendary suns
like phosphorescent spires
in homologous temples "of light"
at the zenith
of electric "angelology"
with the "cities of oppression"
dropping down into the abyss

there then exists
vibration lines
a fount of reticular polar greens
anti-pedagogical structuring technique

a livingness of bold eidetic fires
undercutting the moss of "pomposity" & rouge
as in Miro
with his pre-historic "Cantabrian" pyroclastics *
with his spontaneously modelled curses
against the forgeries of constriction

acuity by membrane
discourse by mixture of Iberia & Dahomey
Miro
with his precise free & cosmic certainty
flowing through thresholds of maturation & demonology
the jagged marmosets & brooks
the isolated blue of miraculous rainbows & seedlings
in an atmospheric spinning akin to "Timur & his lineage" *

then one is illumined
by an image of waves & saffron
by bewildering arabesques of velvet

of course
the animated quintessence of "Behzād of Herat" *
with his "warm" "full" "tones" "for costumes" & "flesh"
at the "zenith" of "Mongol" painting
he who revolted
against dictated stillness
against a dominate calligraphy

what comes to fruit in one's heart
is sublime insurrectionist's blur
bursting from a double set of stars
inspired by phonemic x-rays & heat
by a chronicle of hoaxes
suspended
within impetuous beguilement

then one is ensconced in nervous plurality
as if lost in a fable of "diaphanous" "crickets"
with an apparitional force in the singing of serpents
as if brewed in a hatchery of diamonds

life comes forth
arriving as a skull
scavenging memoirs through a destiny of ciphers
igniting neon lilies
like a "Nilotic" Nubian playing a-priori dice with Parmenides

playing dice
within a hall of ghostly mountain spirals
gambling with holocaust ranges
like an inclement sun
bursting from a gulf of spiders
& the Grecian diablos keeping the score
with diabolical inks & puddings

a victory for rational grief
unlike Carthaginian "popular assembly"

Greece
the first true fish of evil
the first blackened gaze of territorial infants

for Greece
the half of each distance continuously split
as if attempting to land within the confines of Phobos
within its harsh in-fractional risings
always subject
to optimum debility
to microscopic infinitesimals
never arriving
within the scope of articulate dominion
so that the interstice
the map of freshly spilled nacres
becomes a zone invaded
by demonically inverted anathema waters

a "quarantine" of sparks
a decimation of fracto-cumulus frescos

to evolve circles
to flower the arrival of ecto-plasmic borealis
one must paint like a terrifying angel
producing from one's eyes
an alien xenogenesis
from a cluster of dead salmon
this concluded
with a mark of ash
with curved rapier spillage
which turn the teeth into blistering randomness
singing
in dismantled larghettos
in riddled rococo meandering

language in extraneous xenia
in hands of newt
bewitched by intuitive aural lobotomies
hearing across the harmolodium of ether *
across adjacent transient rhyming anomalies
so in the seeds of fabulous stars
one is capable of magical xerophilous

much in keeping
with a "vascular bundle" of rays
capable again
of a high intangible fluorescent velocity

weighing in one's mind
the subjective cracks
the crystalline volcanoes
the crucial percolation of ophthalmic insight

conjunctiva
enabling the absorption of great distance in bodies
enabling Kelvin
by lamb's graft
by exploded hexahedron
by painted dorsal fibrillation
by chants
by cravings
by wood rats

one moves the brush
one arights with the thumb
a disfigured forest on fire
then arkose arises
blanking Euro-colonial polonium blazes

then one announces
the Ceylonese motion of miraculous dragon's blood
its fortuitous & magical hailstone geometry
giving one the voice
the heliotropic blinking sensations

the phosphenes
the burning triangular sundogs in carbon
the hexangular hafniums arisen in trans-finity

one then concludes
alchemical brimstone by ballerina
by nuance
by telepathic parallel intensity

this
the great atmosphere of menace
the prime tropopause of cruelty

so that each canvas one imagines
is suspended in shattered droplets
in simultaneous space
its colour blazing in refraction by spasm
like an isthmus
or a beacon
or a signal in heightened eclipse moray
burning with a force of deleterious nobility
cracking a cathedral of stars with its flame

its imaginal sea
dashing against a rock of glints
against a shore of explosive skuas in flight

one must throw off
an iconography which imprisons
by ideology
by mental canopy which burdens
which dilutes the storms across psychic sunflower seas

& all manner of didactic & heart rate
subsumed in waves of aurora & cobalt
invaded by oars
by boats who breed sea whales

one thinks of haecceity
of thirst
of surreptitious monologue with darkness
its illumined deprivation
alive with engenderment
with circumstantial pauses
with runic hissing anthems
with blackened germinal calligraphies
combined with ores & broken solar dust
so as to reach
the pinnacle
the talismanic ringing mysteriums
the larval ingress of rapacious sweltering dictation
snarling in emerald
in jagged cusp annealments
in blunted micrometer explosions

like a jasmine volcano
like a flashing unsealable methane
shaking
with non-equational proto-spiders
with the first shock of genesis to the womb
with the first unstable pituitary marrows
playing across forms
from the Pre-Cambrian to the Jurassic

expanding in the lightning cells of the spine
as if in herbiferous masquerades
there were forms suddenly formed from eclectic pavonian stillness
as if in the bottoms of a herring cave
there were likenesses spontaneously summoned from brief genetic explosion
like exponential biological cascades
revealing blind human auras in transition
killing & feeding
looking for hooks
for molecules
for indefinite mammals' exudation
so as to fly

with a single sorcerous wing
to an agitated fount
congruent to the Sufic praxis of collection & dispersion

collected on the plane of eternity & light
dispersed across the plane of appearance & suggestion

a great dialysis transfer
nomadic
like a beguiling weed sumptuous with stamina
growing from portions of angelic genetics
with palpable impalpable nerve roots
heating its furnace of strangeness
to a pitch
no longer linked to an armoury of numbers
to a tortuous invidious stasis

perhaps Pollock
with his sensitive burning degenerations
with his clairvoyant passionary threads
brought to a fever
a single conducted voltage
so that ecto-plasmic dreaming was formed
in the white light of space

so in this era of post-eternity
there is the metabolic minus
the functional dysphonia
the moment by moment sheltering germs
straying
like staggered infected bullocks
forgetting their own electrical glimpse of erasure & demarcation

perhaps Pollock
with his fusion & separation of forms
could light the primeval pallors
could give back to Europe its absent alchemical *nigredo*
its lost primeval power of deciphering by sign

but no
Europe peers through corrupt visitation of entrail
cancelling from its personal dogmas
the right of divine cathartic
cancelling
heavenly trans-mixtures
cancelling
the glistening force of Osirian bodily grain

for the Southern psyche
the testing of substance by wild chimerical angelics
by filaments of burning colour & beauty
of gleaming aerial ferocity
of sun ingested eclipse gesture
so that colours are inscribed
on flowing germinal darkness
on solar deluge mescal
on grounds of interior umber

therefore one paints
within a black oasis of comets
emitting spells
of runic Indian parameters
like a surge of soil & sky
blended
along an orange green horizon
implanting yucca & sperm

the boiling moon
the injected rot of ants' saliva
the rigid gas of diurnal Christian bondage
the geo-thermal a-ritual common rulings
the didactic nails on the cross of holy candent murmurs
the unclean force of the monomial missionaries' hatchet

each Indian myth deliberately blinded
scarred with pointless Lutheran survivals
then what ensues is ecological illness
is a mountainous revival of retentive glass enclosure

now
prime necessity calls
for auroral intensity
for teeming sparks & ravines
so that language rises above panic & displacement
& takes in its teeth a fearless infinity of calm
a motionless flight above the soured extremes
excluding saw mills
excluding greenish petroleum mixes
excluding palatial office rigours
yes killing
the bloodless density of measured Cartesian bone
exploded
into transmuted faeces
part fish
part bird
part angel

rituals
which serve one's body with blankness
with penetrant flotational dioramas
with felicity by mime

& so the invisible centrality of Asia
"free swimming" like the "axial" base of the "Sumatran Butterfly Fish"
expanded in a flaring circular garden
alive
in an errorless wave of transcendence

so one paints
the successive modulations
evolved through neutral electrical weight
through seismic hypnotics by glance & eruption

there is paint by disjunctive weaving
by dust from a scalding omphalos
by tempestuous instinct colouration
roving throughout a "Mars Black" ocular line

having the desperate solidity of eggs
capable of breakage
of shattered pinatas & spillage

then the image of Van Gogh
within his stunning cornucopia at Aries
painting Richters in a blazing doll gauntlet
unlike Borinage
where his models bled through furious atmospheres of coal
through dark drizzles of dust
in Aries
there was brightness
there was ritual candescence
there was the fleeting impastos of terror
of Asiatic porcelain & the internal victory of interior Mongol stags

from this there comes to view
melted malachite encircling a flying Dogon's carriage
the transmuting of lizards
into "violet hills"
into "clumps of brambles"
with touches of "yellow" as balance
as for black & white
there are the "twenty seven blacks" of "Frans Hals"
& white
"the highest combination of the lightest red …"

there is the esoteric status of albescence
or the fact
"of neutral coloured paper
which became greenish against a red background"
then "reddish" against a "green"
then "bluish" against an "orange"
then "yellowish" against a "violet"

then the mutual influence of "kindred colours"
of "carmine" / "vermilion"
of "pink-violet" on its violet equivalent of blue

colour transmutes the abyss
takes up its blackened quinine compression
releasing its powers by alchemical expansion
by the continuing diorama of grace

& by grace one means
a conjured volcano of green suns
a burst of black & yellow rapids
a phantom crocodile prairie
a philosophical steed striding orange & blue summits

or a painter awakened in a garret of scarabs
its windows tilted by powerful eclipse foundations
shifted in the air of opalescent ravines
there then arises
an image of heated iguanas
slashing free from a sanguineous mental enclosure
humming a stony jackals' lyric
matching irregular splinters of powder
with Buddhist technique & "Sunyata"

the pigment then blazes
as if the breath were searching for an atmospheric saffron
for a Sybaritic hive

& the eyes
always capable of auras
of seeing by implication & foment
like an irrational flicker of mesons
around a random star or a planet

there then exists insurgence
with its power of fortuitous blinking
with its power of painted rain enigmas

so from the soul of the empty photon shafts
there well up hawks
the awakened Egyptian empirical Ka's
spiralling in mysterious cosmological lustrums

The Stratospheric Canticles

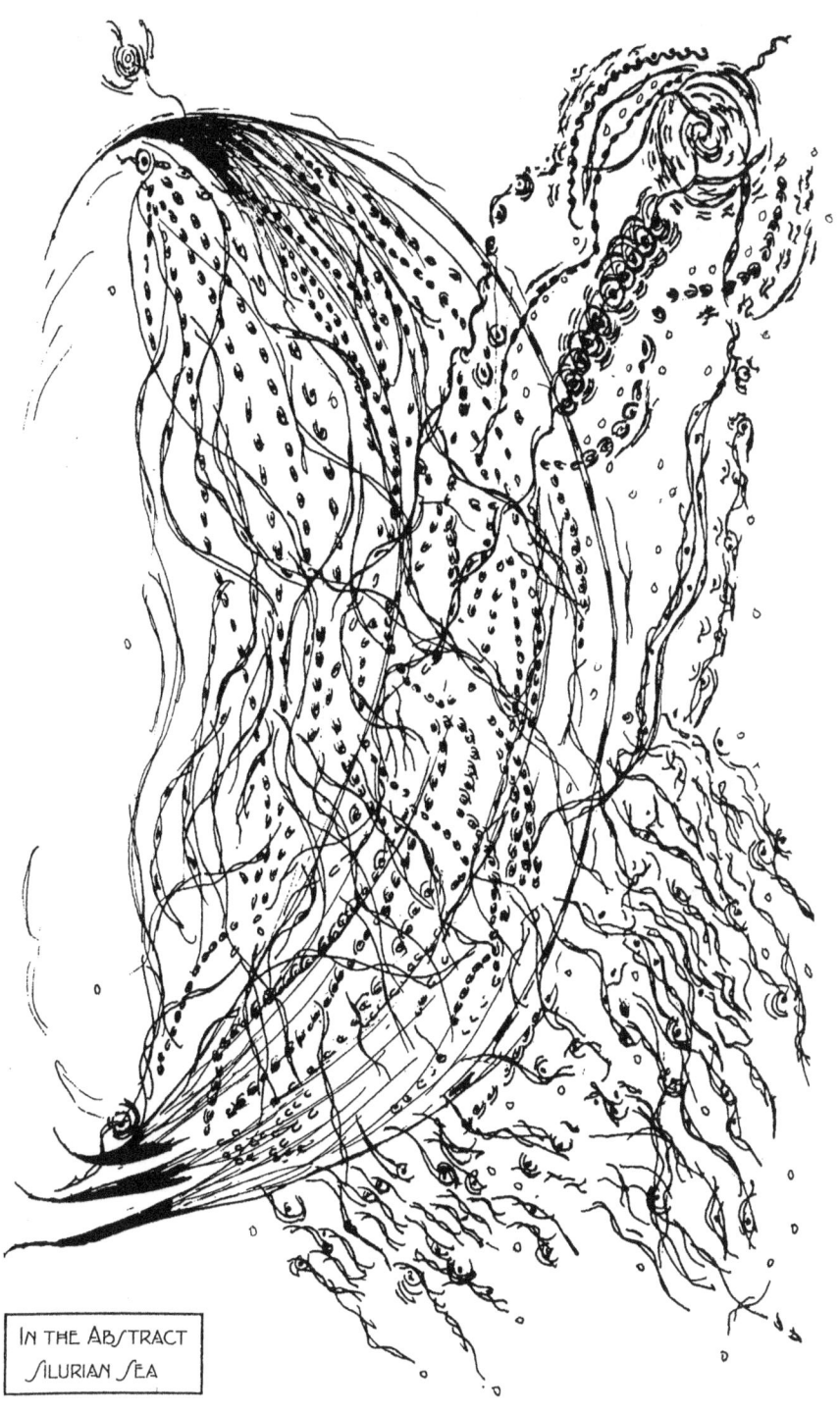

In the Abstract Silurian Sea

like the first thermal Nubians
who seismically centred the sun
who squared the gravity around ghostly proto-planets
who imprinted direction with the fierce harmonias of dawn

so to paint
is to burn in one's earlobes
is to revolve within positional telepathy
so as to soak in the wonder of an atmospheric dread

it is to extract one's calipers
from the aboriginal opposition of rice graves
so as to fuse
one's scattered conducting points
& wake up the metals
in the wild fruition of a savage medial litmus
a thirst
a winding intuitive blood salt
a conduct soaked in flaming neural pragmatics

so that one paints with a stroke of atavic neuron tornados
with a blow of magical phlogiston thickets

so that
an object is multi-lateral
condensed
altitudinous
stratospheric
open

Impulse & Nothingness

Impulse & Nothingness

These dense geranium surges of thought
protracted through steaming anthrax waters
concerned with the coronal aspects of contingency
those sabbatical athanors in which nothingness looms
without image
without the doctrinal plumage of a fixed event
without the mesmeric square of Talmudic rigidity
when one is transfixed by intention
by the Messianic force fused with the illusive intensity
of impulse
shot into the grainy broach of nothingness

there exists the sense of bleached equators
the suicidal aching of secondary sunfish

one then gives off the odour of a pentecostal heresy
& one no longer lives in an aura of the weakened
with the weakened
one stands like a bolt
upright
facing the electrical debris of an ochlocracy in pain
staggered by the knife of its own surgeon's riddles
by a rabid scalpel cutting at its ribs
by a deboned pleurisy rumbling in its vision

as I reach into this nothingness
I am abandoned by associates
psychically spat upon by contemporaries
a reflex
against one condemned by the interests
of the secular nerve field

this I
a target
with an intense circulation of acid in the veins

so everything that I snare
always half plunged into eclipse
all my description
subject to electro-ballistical analysis
an analysis of my own achievement
which ironically has no power to engulf me

so I remain suspended
between light & the imageless arcana of extinction
& the emotions
those electrical cadavers
weave themselves like a sickened medicine in my thorax

as to my name
it has become an exploded raven's dyscrasia
an excrescence
walking around with my eyes
like a series of neurological sunspots

& in speaking
I remain corroded with intensive tedium rejoinders
with my bones squirming at an angle of pathological
nightmare edicts
a cauldron of metacarpal tsunamis
as a result
I feed on the carking magnificence of loneliness
on the nomadology of cacti & sores

I count my companions as enemies
those obedient nomenciators covering up those abbreviated
prolusory murders of the spirit
& so as a scar
as one given up to the guerrilla domain of
cosmic prolepsis
I am always a figure
a metal hormone found in a basket
floating on broken seabird's blood

on both sides of my eyes a parenthetical numbness
a painful but voided exogen climacterics
in which I wander through intensive flytrap grasses
weaving myself to death while humming in-doctrinal ballets
a shapeless fumatory witness
suffering like a cipher
or a metamorphic anagram
spying on shapes in the darkness

Utopian Parallel Intensity

No longer annealed to transplanted erosion
to circumspect armouring channels
with swirling boron effluvia
peering into sundered quotidian ethics
allowing a virginal mercury
a penetration through samsaric connivance
making me parallel
with utopian stellar intensity

so that
a vessel of quail
brazen
precise
fluidic
no longer hails me
no longer burns me with fictitious gnome digestion

at times
me
the ingracious brigadier
part antelope & sand
upright in the morass
like a chronicled infant
singing out
in oblivious solar incantation

the cathartic pain ingestion
the tedious mud invention
peering over a powerful lethargy of wounds
like a rainbow of scars connected to immensity
to deeper inebriation
no longer a brush
with Byzantine cataracts under "Isidorus the Younger" *
with murky Darlingtonias *
with the obsession of John Cade *
with the coded calendrical blackness of Assyrian enunciation

my hands blowing
through pillaged asteroid asylums
spelling out fire in a sea of treacherous monsoons
with intense lexigraphical archeries
allowing me
only the high moral catharsis of language
ironic
as the flames of deconstructed knitting manuals
I have survived
the cold American debacle with its gauntlets
with its niggling bludgeoner's edicts
which always
around the scarf of its soundings
seeks to code a list of its various judicial indictments

but always on guard
against assassination & hookworm
my aura exists
above propane & discord
above linear scansion & its cell salts
destroying the paralytic
of secular integers & judgement

Rays from the Biographic X-ray Chalice

A barometer
of tense hormonal spillage
watching
my character twist like a
watchdog
splintered
by a chromosomal looking glass
at times
cloudy
as if under the law of defective
tellurian spasms
nightingale bickerings
inside
my violet china cabinet deltas
as if
in the rotary blizzards of love
the chainsaw clingings
had multiply arisen
fully osculate
in a smouldering bed of bioluminescence
as if
gliding under a moon of fire
the lover
as an x-ray chalice of squid
her thighs
like powerful female uranology
like miraculous erasures & resurrections
like driftwood & grenadine vocal dementia
like marine worms
sucking fevers from exquisite pantomime interiors
because
to feel the dialectical pleasure of fire
is galactic
so I say

the galaxies burn in my sperm
my lungs
like salacious Caligulan erotics
upon a barge
of hideous jewellery & dust
like a steaming blasphemer's mirage
I float
beneath the nebular force of Outer Mongolian mirrors
the woods
geometrically burning on Callisto *
in the singular match of the sun
a Taoistic staircase exploding
door by door
as exquisite intuitive indifference
therefore
like a hair lip
like uranium tattoos
vomiting up mange into the edicts of Kant
into inky acacia mirages
under a chartreuse malediction
under a bevy of skies
placing
the swirl of my psyche
into hazy infernos
into the ultimate thickets
of kinetic molten & lust

The Recidivous Concubine of Dimness

To take a well whipped stone
from the roof of your eyes
from your splintered medlar poppies
& hold it in front of your blackened optical chords
like a penetrant mirror of fire

giving body to your dispassionate withdrawal
reflecting your weakness
your insidious tomb of adynamic carnality
you gall me
you seek to reify my tense tornado linguistics
to plunge me into shaking pre-iguana disconnection
to stammer in limbo
to turn away from my blood
so as to swallow indigestible abstracts
sucking into my lungs crippling fumaroles of anguish
so that I stumble around
wiry and in-illuminant
deprecated
burdened
as if you had slashed up a moon of whiskey in your sleep
as if you had turned your pelvis into a frozen
chastity anchor
a creaking skeletal adumbration
obnoxious calamander burning
releasing crystals & soot from your minimal
glandular apparitions
you are that jaundiced dust
full of felonious gnostic hairs gone sour
like amnesial wandering straw
like dictated briars & rotted acetate primevals
like illusional radium on a defeated sea of
turpentine & glare
you never inspire in me
jasper or diamond
but odiferous holocaust lepers & rabies
bird spells
sharded Pre-Cambrian anaemias
when I call you answer with
cancerous palm oil
with psychotic elderberries
because you eat at my patience by dulling me with echoes
with those indefinite mourning pellets
with those diluted cherries & lavas
you encumber the cranium

with mismatched horror & tonics
each time I ask you to stand you fail me
it seems you want loneliness to circuitously
ooze from my pores
so that I accept a negative spider's screaming
walking with my head dropped
into a dangerous breathing of vipers
dejected
sun blanched
staggering through a shattered bay of diamonds
always waking up in darkened brooding gowns
moment after moment
the brain cells wizened
by an inescapable creosote hatchery
you
the recidivous concubine of dimness
plaguing me with obnoxious diagonal riddles
you
wanting to keep me in lugubrious proximity
planting cross storm peppers in my aura
you
keeping my moments doubled over with phobia
with supercilious reduction
with savage botulism pyres
you
with the covetous strychnine angles
with varnished methane cataracts & boundaries
I renounce you
you
with the wicked insulin saliva
cancelling
your pockmarked misdemeanour hull
with fumes
in a secretive vegetal sclerosis

Entropy as the Bone Queen

Always smoking inside my skin
with your nagging territorial stamens
with your chronic teutonic measuring worms
always coughing up snakes under sun-embargoed Baobab trees

your nostrils corroded by lobotomy & brine
with a history of horrified mortality incisors
your breasts like scarlet bracts
like illegible muscatel
full of steaming melancholia in your braids
the wick of terrified lactation
stagnant
burning
at the very source of luminescence
wrangling
with prorogation & debasement

never enough for you to dwell on aurelian turquoise
or spell out your name in jasmine or diamonds
for you
a barrier of umlauts
a baked Germanian Sahara
a zoological spasmodic
a zone of missed propositions & foreboding

of course you are hiding your soaked New Guinean arrows & curses
your cracked neurological abutments
wanting to turn on me a poisoned fan of arrowheads
to shower me with a cunning dyslogistical oblivion
am I beleaguered by such analogical terror?
by your shifting transmutations studded by icy warhorse mirrors?
scurrilous
shaking seismological propane above my skull?

never giving to you advantage
never lofty terrorist morsels

not even the kernel of a common Renaissance blemish
expecting me to mount exquisite dwarf rotundas
with the power of auricular happenstance

there is flat refusal & scandal
there is the night
under a green demonic belly
swarthy
overcast
without reticular sobriety
to procreate its atoms
to live in its thirst
in its leanest microbial core

therefore
under a zodiacal Andromedan lean-to
under a fierce ghostly angular furnace
there is rage
there is unforeseen aggression
in that ancillary state vocally assembled as surcease
which riddles in essence the Stygian eclipse
with its icy parenthetical motifs
which makes it stagger
& forget its first hallucinated motives
its first dyspeptic procedure

this is love
this is the true fertility of the bone nest
the true in-combinatory cogito
the cherished crystallization
which electrocutes each of your poisoned necromancer's tribes
your geriatric fate
hiding the face of a star
dreaming & re-dreaming
throughout transformative abruptness & dying

this is love
ensconced in spectacular photino exclusion
the natural non-conveyable bullion

the sunlit rubidiums
the blighted ingress lodges
elevated
above the wounded silk of embossed doctrinal noises

because in your existence there is no practical purpose
no hallucinogen to honour the uncircumcised glintings
reflected down into the limitless gullets
connecting anti-being & being
connecting
the weakened marsupial ghostliness
those collective spirals of ghostliness
with presence as essential nublado

The Monsoon Queen of the Soul

Up in these enriched
uranian lobotomies
one sees the sky
whirling through gentian lunar destruction
its burning
asteroidal dislodgments
its vatic cranial blizzards
scattered like a centaur
galloping across sundials
transmuted by flooded oracular vertigo
into a Queen
burning in her voluptuous rhinestone habits
imaging in her dreams
Andromedan skull mirages
implying indelible blood skins
breathing Saturnian fumes above flaming
heretical meridians
imploring in her chartreuse galactic mandalas
a galaxy of volcanic sundrops
cast into the violet dawns of psychic

aerial combat
mountainous crystalline combat
conducted in a chariot of fiery
skeletal snow
a Queen
in a palace of emeralds
seeking the key to bleak
hermetical moraines
exploding on a plane of
omniscient seeds & luminescent planetary bregmata
no
not the melodramatic anthills
not the urinated peppertrees
screaming
dense
sonic configurations of ligneous harlots & seizures
not the bird dung
not the raft of migrating personal delusions
ejected from the plans
of violent embryo erotics
but the soul
the inky minimal cypress
brought to bear
within the floating devastations
of erupting coral monsoons

Call to My Flaming Starfish Shakti

Perhaps
with sardines and bribery
with a mud fish
with a grove of lunar
pre-induction cherries
with a love of splintered muskrat corrals
with eclipse sandals
& mockery

with a fully wrought
neon rabbit
I seek to anneal you
with my clockwork eyes
with my surreptitious moth kidneys
because
I must bring you to me
I must walk into the waves
of your tenacious clitoral pulling
sleeping with my skull
wide open
yes
a sleeping valve
an aboriginal phonetics
implanted by the bony grains of radium in your teeth
awakening in my mouth
a comprehensive brain scan
intense neutrino ivies
shaking in the depths
my bloody quail's oil magic
my sinister documentary ardour
giving me
the power to burst
these hard baronial confines
aching for you
my flaming starfish shakti
with your Amazonian lips
leaning from your castle
of pylons & rubies
with your necklace of froth & saliva
walking your inaugural caimans
through waves of imaginal cerulean humanity
your Tunisian integument
blazing like a Martian river
in the blackness
your eyes
part cinnabar
part malarial & tungsten
your hair

both verdurous & dolphin's blood
always sucking the smell of berries
from your nostrils
always silver floods
& canine volcanoes
you
the magnetic starquake
the crimson Sultana
oozing
from your nails
meridianal deposits
of graft & disjunction
those merismatic habits
those chartreuse breaths
those gulfs of spectacular
piscatorial bleaches
spectra of coal dust
of vituperative hydrogen
angles
blooming in magnesium funnels
in the black oasis
of the genes
empowered by impulse
by the purity
of henna & nothingness

Oblique Sensorial Savagery

You are green
with gainful hair trigger plumage
with pangs of ice to fathom
like a rookery of seas
totemic with abstract coffin powder

& so your savagery
under powers of perpetual connivance

blinding with censure
with rude fascistic bottlebrush criteria

which keeps the subconscious ingrown
the angelic dharma darkened
your red hair curling
like voluptuous cobras under fire
like tungsten candles
like flares
& chemical Bedouin rubies

every savage green dawn
your stinging gecko bracelets
as if
you had sundered whales with your steps
as if
under the thorns of the moon
you had sent up a plastique of cherries
those emerald mongoose auras
those living stochastic fan worms
seeking to cover
torrential spillage from your navel
as if
under the heated whip of day
I would switch your voltage
to pluperfect intrigue
to a deeply lined mascara
to hot Babylonian salamander gardens
watching you amble
through greenish sodium flames
making molten rise & fall
turning the far-flung poles into vapour

in this psychic Shangri-la
my jealousy generates
your copulation with tigers
because one can never measure
the dangerous impact
of your skull on fire with penultimate transparency

I witness your chunks of flesh
on swirling turpentine carpets in hell
tossing back & forth
the pressure of stingrays
the disdainful panic
fused in bleak omega laundries

your moonless hormone slaver
like darkened signals
like glazed tornado herrings
like blank leukaemia invective

from tragic tables of skin
I glimpse your glowing morphine copper
your tense Cambodian chemise
always implying meteorites & osmosis
always cooking in your nostrils
a wayward blend of hot photinos & selvas

Subtractive Venery

Calling me
with your sickly rhomboid status
calling for me
to return to your insomnial wisteria palace
to your overnight guano dimension
to suck on your simulated jasmine
erected by your barrier of chastity by furnace

your cadaverous wrenching of fate
your lobotomized smouldering of dislodged confusion
your incapable tarantula piddling
plaguing me with purgatorial cratering analysis

with your diet of melted swan's food
starving me

always checking my semen
with frantic dyslexic syllables of dread
with your tortuous hounding
with your repetitive scratching of conscience
trying to hold me with scarring
trying to clamp my brain with geriatric forceps
with ligatures of wire
with stony mollusc rims & serrations

in this you have failed
you have invalidated your dysfunctional efforts
of innocence
of perverted virginity
with a mangy face before the eye of God
not even summations of crawling
not even rust cutters or combustion
as if to test your blue vaginal mirrors
inside a Protestant Crimea
listening to your fallacious absorption neurosis

you've forfeited your flames
you've cast into the moat
salacious bonfire bathing
you've given up the power of deepened torturing rums
of magnetic chromosomal nerves
for a weekly neutered clairaudience of failure

in my mind
those ghostly Bermuda funnels
always invading your trajectory
with shattered mercurial caresses
which makes your heart exfoliate
into multiple Appaloosas
into stony aerial confusion
churning
desperate
hyperactive
with momentary chartreuse injections in your system

so I've become oblique to you
you've made me want to annul
the nasal
the spiral spinning jennies in you

you've borne in on me
with dust grapes
& I've triumphed above a contradictory wall
above the burning
the torment
the seizures

and so
bony with rickets & prefigured decay
you've forgotten the sun
wandering across deserts of air
never once hot
with intercourse & reddish rhinestone habit

you've passed on the chance
to fly as a deeply bloodied heron
above a newly focused sodium sea
you've passed on the adventure
of fleeing through the gore-flecked bounty of yellowed maritime grasses
to wallow on a couch
magically multiplied into pluperfect brothels
into an ambience of greenish radium & silver
calling out to the plentiful ghosts
of erotic turpentine & nothingness

chewing owls' flesh
witnessing the shredding of mimetic eglantine murals
those powders of kinetic jugular bliss
allowing us a proto-immersion
allowing us a winged ensconcement
in the very core of hellish underwater gravel
you've renounced
with your peculiar ethical subtraction
the blue corn of light

the hot tornado plumage
alive
with the verdurous intensity
of paradise & flaming

Candle from the Black Widow's Love Cake

Your inherited terminations brought to bear
at the spark of our excited destinal embrace
in the fiery zone of our embroidered cabarets

& when you are absent
when our mutual burnings split apart
it's as if you had flitted
to a transparent Montparnasse
or a magical helium Sicily
or a transposed coronal Algeria

your sensuous gas
blowing through the mist of Chaldean water trees
leaving me
taking your dense
recalcitrant iguanas
my plural identity breaking
as if I had become a self-created hireling
a cyclone of mustard
full of heterotaxia & weeping
& just as magically you return to me
after the ache
of my prolonged unbearable insomnia
having brought you back
with my divinatory incisors
with my snow-white emperor moths
breaking cobra's eggs over fire

breaking through my casement of sulphur
with your ungracious iguanas
squealing like electric serpentine cadavers
raw
with oligarchical voltage
the sun cut off in their hearts
inflicted with notorious hatchlings of larvae
crucibles of liver uvulitis & terror
wicked with the moans of lariats & frustration
each iguana
speckled with windburns & powder
in the spectacular nerve of their anger
expecting each eye to explode
expecting during each of their woundings
to be devoured by riddles
summoned from the conflicted torture of Mercury
because
your lips of softened iron
the insidious meadowlark prairies in your bosom
the scorched ejections
the lava of your taunting clitoral vials
playing with plummeted tactical arias
with the naked crafts of lice
with a cryptic virgin radiography
as if
in the cave of each iguana scar
there were a beehive of scalps & spurtings
my divinations
burning in the glass of my runic pituitary mirrors
within the parenthetical glimpse of typhoon & nutmeg
reciting stammers from an aleatoric treatise on sunbeams
I greet you at the gorge of tangled wildebeest betrayals
our lips merging
like parallel electron tornadoes
like ironic Uranian ignitions
like a spiral of sizzling urinal wires

a potent phlogiston current
with blistered moth equators

Impulse & Nothingness

with abrasive parakeet smelters

& your iguanas
Lotapes & Lucifer *
hissing gallstones candles & sugar
& your face
"lighted by the ... fumes of a poppy
thrown on live coals"

you seek to distress me
with obverse discomforts
yet my addiction
fearful of becoming a masculine Oenone *
fearful of tumbling from my fiery silicate erosion
from my wavering prepositional errata
from my distinctive ventriloquial algebraics
as to strontium lenses
as to the loquacious fire of the logos
I think of our ignitable citron embraces
our geometric & Hebrew embraces

& we emerge from all of this litmus
as strangers
like muscatel
like heated tungsten fractures
strangely melodious
like hyperemian fragments
laced with the night

To My Savage Muscatel Lady

(for Jayne Cortez)

A burst of connivance & bluish medical
sorcery & cramping
torturing your lips
with the harsh salt of irony

burning in a bed of wood salt
& love
stamens glancing your cheeks with
flaming decibel grains & ivy
as if I were a matador
being miraculously honed
by your smouldering cobalt screws
by your hardened toenail laundry's
flapping
in a golden rubidium breeze
your lips of blood
seismic
with ulterior itching
& scandal
with lobotomies
motivated by cyanide
& dripping
you bathe me
in your breath of speckled ultramarines
& cobras
your holistic rapier embrace
like a glance of yellowed cadmium spurs
always
a looming Ovadia orange swelling
in your mouth
a looming muscatel fragment
ready to scald me
with hypnotic gale storm needles
with erupting plesiosaur's ironics
if I love you
it is because
I am wild with hammered
cockscrew ointments
ready
to give you
a blossom of wires
with goatskins
with coded optical brine
with love in a nest of

rudely practiced viper's keys
with graft paper
with haemorrhages suddenly choked
by the slaver of the sun
so that the planets
the astrological winters
like a gum tree
like a hypochondriac magically sawing
his stilts with grains
like a quilt of snake & oil investments bleeding
with the moss of herbiferous decades
like a stamp or a wolverine
because
in each of my five senses
I love you
with the power of resurrected phosphorus
or a tenacious skua on fire
therefore
we must hide in tunnels of bickering
in stony negative cartouches
in an armed camp
sucking on branded rhubarb babies
bonded to the squeaks of disastrous
lemming upheaval
always halted
always neck biting & birdseed
always under smoking fever germs
the inevitable stickler's rot
the war paint
the depleted ozone mummies
simply to stick
a rose in your skull
simply to inscribe a painless
hooking dowel on your navel
like a crab
all pink
all savage
all girlish with muscle

Wavering Rumination on Ontology

Taking out the guts
of death
with witchcraft athanors
with the art of floating salmonella explodents
with the wings of imaginary uranian vultures
to yearn for visions of haunted
radon summations
surges of tubercular barleys
tonnage proposals
a mirror strapped
to silver-plated molecule incisors
like a shark or a star
cankerous
tumultuous
oceanic
grown
boll weevil's solution
a tank of cream-coloured lilies
weaving
like a bird devoured by traitorous amoebas
as if asked to give a perfect account
as if to justify one's cowardice
one's self-inflated vomit
because
I know no vomit
I know no leonine felt
no leonine tracheotomies
the throat of logic
listless
as if it were dying
on its last bed of ropes
snapping out
at fractured havens of grace
its sexless multiplicands
its droseric Pandora's whims
tied

to the inky corals
to raven-coloured bonnets
of bubonic haematopias
me
I seek the brilliant sundown edicts
the burst
of spasmodic claustrophobics
in a magnetic hail of sudden
sexual love

Remorse & Infinity

Rushing into salt
& blackened sapphire shadows
immortality
like exploded chandeliers
like loosened Babylonian grave stockings
floating
into immortal oregano auroras
as lobotomies
as mitotic pound crystals
those gressorial landfills
those gressorial asylums
burning
like yellowed astral coral
across eclectic neutron grasses
each biological ark
a meteor
a rotating cellular frenzy
as a glass pagoda of germs
holding at an angle
exotic millimetre winds
each eye
a mango
a violent penetration of blackness
a living dracaena body

a stuttering chartreuse agenda
in blond incessant mirror gardens
swirling
in a hot green mother wind
in embattled micro-terror
as blank neutrino species
as hidden mildew sparrows
so everything bends
like an orchard of blinding guttural rinses
of sunburned cryptology
emerging from a morgue of dissembling tornadoes
their hands
bickering with giants
with pestilential crustacean mirages
attempting to live through the fervour of panic
in a listless marigold agrology
full of asters & squid
extracting from the neural field
fiery Orphean rums
yes
dialectical flakes
of remorse & infinity
those deeply cankered germinal debilities
as a mark of gas
as silver mytheme orations
like an angelic burst
into an amoral falling
of hyperemian rains

The Vaporous Cortical Field

Partially spewed
from magnetic uterine deltas
like paint frothing
from generic fish & declension
disrupting

proportional tedium
with magic semen murals
condensed
with penultimate finality & glass
& so the cobalt explosions
the purple mandrake glaring
into cadmium apparitions
trampling harridan foundations
voracious
inspirational scarlets
the terminal orchids
& bland placenta riddles negated

prime integers
poetic lightning & fog
in fact
smoking nebula & eaglets
those lighted diagonal crab pots
subjectively riddled
with all the gold of subliminal transfusion
those polygamous moralities
the wild courageous maulings
the inscrutable architect's vapour
flying out
from malleable turpentine castles
again cadmium apparitions
on a series
of spectacular blood steeds
charging Venusian gas & dust
smouldering Renaissance persimmons
vacillations
crushing Teutonic Lord games
escaping the early mineral crawlings
of Masaccio
I think of abstract jonquil battalions
those ultramarine liberations
those hot siennas of flux
implying anodyne vultures
a truculent ardour

a dark Numidian ire
hornets splashing
magical rhomboid yellows
triangle ices
studding
liquifous bardo chapels with brightness
blown-up Vatican frescos
like
a voice of green hound dogs
imprinting pivotal moths
& instinctive
electrical neurosis
somniferous mantras
blending into a red violet light
into a plethora
of Prussian blues & limes
into a seething micro-hypnosis
into a cherished assault of preconscious
terrors & bleeding

those mean infernal salvos
those arachnoidal bone spinnings
a lunging skeletal psychosis
a monstrous saturnine oblation
in a field
of vaporous cortical infinity

Augury

A bird
floating above
a fiery delta of blood
diamantine
voracious
eclectically haunted
by poisoned spells & runes
in lands of proto-Hominidae

Dauntless Cimmerian Farming

In this garden
of torrential x-ray foliage
I scatter leptons & brandy
wasted germinal diamonds
forcing black enigmas to grow
coaxing with voltage
vertical solar intangibles
hypnotic hydrogen collapses
magnetic occult amphibolics
mined from a sigil
within a curious basking
brewing as a doctrine
an insidious stellar oasis

Bewitchment from the Radium Furnace

Its gaze
its mark
like the anti-diurnals of wakeless ingestion
with a glowing & traitorous smoke

as an opera sung beneath the ruse of an invincible belladonna
or a Belgian trader pleading with treacherous ivory
about the effects of the lethal waves on his hands
with his fingers
of calendrical red poppies
dissected
like a coded neon forest
with his pulse producing eyes
like an in-fluorescent barley
their corruption alight

& intensively curved by posterior demon
he is marked from prehistory
by a wall of dissolving glucose metrics
craving a bordello of swine
or a tubercular haunt
of aching powder harems & necrotic libido
unlike the work of the Senegalese miner
he speaks
with a sickened caliper of French
like neutered dice in a sperm bank
or a cranial kind of whiskey
part skin
part badgering of thirst
he trades in claws
in a worldview of plutonics
scooping eyes from cooked millet
the marks on his hands
from the furnace of a contained radium summary
erroneously announcing
the coming myth
of the Polar Bear as leper
as imported clarion mathematics
turned to an eclipse of salvos

a brutality
not unlike
libellous anorexias
prebiotic marks & scales
assumed in molecular urns
in the social dearth of rotted banking clauses

the Belgian evolves a system
of eating difficult grams of Roman salts & puddings
or having comets mathematically bleed
from a clinical & loathsome harassment

his astrology of descent
Pluto in Vega
ganglionics in beta-Capricorn

in league with the five descending centuries of Nilotic alienation
like a squared barometer of grief
he pounces upon calculation
but his birthmarks
his negative cornucopias
enigmatically strangled in the sullen blood of mystery

Between History & Omniscience

Breathing
insomnious magical tornadoes
insomnious feldspar orations
blown across the sun by blazing Nubian ellipse

this hot accessorial nothingness
where the blood takes wind like a subset of vultures
like powdered rubies or ether

always confronted by this intensive Nubian ellipse
with this bleak abscission of illusion
I speak of expressive calendrical flaws

of jagged Thracian toxicity
spilled
as the bloody geraniums of Normandy *
of Nelson
of Marathon
of Smolensk
of My Lai

yes
the medical floors of war
the progressive marasmus
the listless mental scars
on the roving brow of the Roman Marcellus *

here I am
like a wheel bug
with a "piercing proboscis"
commentating in crow
tropophilous
sinistrodextral
rinsing my being
of prejudicial dialectics
no longer corralled
by a mausoleum of amoebas
of bone thrills
of acidic incensement
of token marsh indoctrinations

a transmundane momentum
blowing beyond
a syllogistical burst
neither luminosity or fatigue
purged of traitorous flatworm insignias
seeing deeper
with the power of anisometropia
against Mark Anthony & Kutozov *
against the seeming heraldic banditry of a Rommel in the desert *

all of them abstersions
transparent abstersions
illusional derelictions
"Lysander in the Aegean" *
"Scipio's Utica & Zama campaigns" *
"Bonaparte's scheming Austerlitz campaign"

in the end
war
that deadly condition of blood & errata
whose sensorial grip
is tensely erased
by miming momentous suns
smoking in the meat of utter recess & magic

of green Wigginsia & jeopardy
at the human core of the transparent astral

as if I saw myself with hives
with Red Pagoda flowers
with burning Arcimboldoesque catacombs
emptied of time-bound optical wounds
slipping along the slopes of a slivered infinity
full of ghostly photinos & snow
as if they were guano
& edicts
& rum
as if they were dove smoke & Ritalin
as if they were mongoose lanterns
exploding through incessance

& all the Mandarin self-reduction
& all the icebergs
with the white Deinonychus wailings *
climbing trilobite pulleys
into high arterial gardens
those iodine systems
those simple darknesses
which cause invincible voltage to snare
triggering a poisonous centrix of thought
warped as monstrous lineal congestion
as emperic disaster
as when Napoleon
unable to quell his blasphemous lobotomies
his insidiously crowned diabolical lobotomies
haunted his own veins
by concussively splaying ghosts across distance

his testament
like a Reichian vegetal obstruction
with the human instinct blurred
by dense collusional winds
by heightened mercurial fraud
by incapable Venusian fire

then
the greater more swallowing stars obscured
by herrings
by quotidian poltergeist intensities
with even sleep compounded by numerical sweat mirages

because
each fragment of land:
homicide
each equitable killer:
leader of the country
all parts
of the dominated polis:
failure

therefore
Himmler *
with his broken civilian asperation
trying to foresee
a standing army in the Pleiades
but the SS *
a fractured animal wave
a mist of general psychic wreckage
casting static monomial dice into flailing

such is history
subconsciously liminal
like a summoned snake across a riddled sea of gerunds
or like a cougar attempting to claw
at the philosophic worms in fertile Nubian ground
at its essence
at its elliptical afferent
yet always shadowed
by its cougars' flaming neural boundaries
its eaten alchemical retardation
like penultimate culmination
like wayward hemlock daggers
sculpting Hitler's icy slaughters in a sullen cubistic Stalingrad *

yes history
as nude non-agrarian horror
centred upon dried colloquial barley
stunted
by flags & tombs
by leaders with implanted blood in their bosoms
always the political act
the warped social blunting
the blinded venereal dollars
scattered
irresolute
like a virus
keeping the personality implanted with extrinsic samsaras
calling up extinguished faces of carnivorous skeletal neurotics
floating face-up in a river of negative cadmium detumescence
electrocuted pigment
morose genetic dissemination
like a darkened chemical synopsis
projected into the role of cold tamasic as error
history being prone
to dictated binding

& for the living
always pressure
always the brain cells fighting entropy & stultification
fighting off death
fighting off the memory of Judaic legal houndings
always triggered within the foci of combat
the theocracy of knaves
the deadly intestinal logos
no longer a great cryptographic deflection
from a tracheal Nubian transparency

in contrast
magnetic feldspar rhythms
a dexterous nova of swans
a garden of black honey on fire
these are the forces
the utopias which mingle in indefectible omniscience

above the weight of blazing centaur trepidations
above the wavering of a seismic galactic damnation
brought to bear upon heavenly monsoons
of uranic optical rotation

The Final Poltergeist of Pompeii

In this ruthless zone of nervous brutality
all the pleasures
fiery
Draconian
vociferous
I sit
eating magical polyps in a Pompeiian mercury shop
finding myself green
astrally elusive
an invisible proleptic enigma
seeking to make the dead take heed
to make the dead wake up & listen
as they suck through their nostrils
rich consumptions of chickpeas & vomit

the patricians boarding Soso's piscatorial motifs *
their genital hairs perfumed with lascivious saffron
& myrrh
with a clandestine cynical rot

it is the day before Vesuvius
& giant hogs are slaughtered for numerous triclinia
& me
the poltergeist
shattering goblets
invisibly screaming
then magically slithering along the "Street of the Tombs"
to the rancid mirage of the feasts
where the women

with the sex of earthquake broaches
with a lust for suckling pigs & goblets of blood
their nipples arrayed
with wet pieces of silver
perhaps
at the villa of the Tauris'
or the Porcius'
or the Aper's *
feasting on spicy moray & mullet
their mouths
always spiny with anticipated carnage
discussing the exploits of Brebix & Nobilior *
reading a list from common murdering tablets
the instinctive labial twitchings

eyeing the buttered snails & the "beheaded birds"
while sipping on strong Falernian wines

& me
the poltergeist
faintly leech-coloured
my transparent ions burning with prolepsis
attempting to nudge their shoulders
with strangely mephitic gusts
yet nothing exists except indifference & bribery
the gambling schools
an ace of dice called "the throw of dogs"
wagered for sesterces & silver

& I flit along the "broad flags of travertine"
inside the Pompeiian Forum
its northern end propled with literal apparitions to Juno & Minerva
with my invisible citron optics
I see the spacious exchange of the "priestess
… Eumachia"
the butchered crows at the bloody *macellum* *

& me
the poltergeist

flitting down the Strada dell' Abbondanza
to the Strada Stabiana south to the Caserma dei Gladiatori
watching the killers practice blows to the urinary organs
the stench of the unruly gladiators' barracks
all of them doomed
having no eyes to see me

then flitting to the baths
to the *thermae*
the prostitutes swarming the *tepidarium*
their bodies adorned with jewellery & crab
heated by Venusian oysters & tumult
always in their eye
the fact of capital gain & slaughter
an imposing whore belching an eel from her thorax
another spewing figs from the creams of her life organ
& the talk is of butchery & terror
of freshly spilled intestinal seas

& I ramble the diaspora of the mansions
screaming in terse intuitive Latin
instinctively haunting
the lodgings of Sallust *
of the "Golden Cupids"
of the "Silver Wedding"

& me
the poltergeist
full of psychic curiosity
watch the buildings of "Sarno limestone" weaken
in their final scintillation of opprobrium & malice
the day before Vesuvius
a crescendo of routine & blankness
of rude stomping in the arena
of crass imperial comfort like a disease of ironic ammonia

& me
the final poltergeist of Pompeii
screaming at the last sun breaking up in the sea

at the last imported barbarity of tigers
at the last nepotistical confetti of political blackmail
& harassment

now frantic
now flitting through the Porto Ercolanese *
listening to the dead volcano groan
sprinkling acid on the revellers at Fannius Synistor's *
waiting for the sun to blow open
for the lava to flow & turn the flesh into tufa

Grasp at an Unknown Existence

A group of blown Hominidae
caught within the blaze of smoking hemlock typhoons
with their contradictory fishhook sparks
each Hominid grasping for existence
for a perceptible grammar of clots
while clawing
& heinously disappearing
by predilection in the asteroids
by destiny as spontaneous iridium gulf
as each deathly ache
transpires in the offspring
in an in-built resistance
burning
as a conundrum of wounds
of sightless trespassers' swarming
upon the perch of a luminous heresy
upon the speech of unknown stalactites
more brimming
more insidious than the throat

An Odd Neuteria

When particles concur across a catastrophic balance
it is the odd conjunctive
like a deadly line of wolves
or a mimicked or timorous radium tree
or a quavering lantern
or an isometric law

in fact
one reveals
a base conjunction
where ciphers accrue
which crowbars ignite & dismantle
with a thirst
part star
part psycho-telluric

where deficits burst
where methodics enkindle
like perfidious ingestion
garishly disembodied by day

therefore
a life of perpetual gall
a starved & wandering apprehension
meteoritic by inch & node
part termite wood
part owl by staggering balletics
part dice in a basin of eclipsed sierras

Hellenistic Camouflage

Dark obsessional rivulets
whispering androgyne rotation
whispering from the throat of ennui

that the dead can see by faith
by their opaque engagement of fever
charismatic with harangues
with possession of a crown of angelic ailments
hung in a zone of mythological displacement
like a spiral of infected mountain ghosts
where camouflage distends
ignited on a fleeting ice plateau

The Rising Eye

I have given myself
carnivores to sleep with
carking Sphinxian
dioramas to relate to
yet
from the pit of the soul
the eye is rising
like a declivitous flight of vertical auroras

Volatility

Taking off
with sudden synesthesial ciphers
to a magical jasmine star
across untold radii
& subsets of blankness
the evolutive prothesis
touching its essence
its burnings
its heart marks
at the torrential pivot of daily diurnal drownings

Alchemic Moray's Reversal

With banishment
there came lust
there came algor
there came the exile of crags
a general moray's malingering
like incelestial encampments
on a Danube ensconced with tedious icebergs & kindling
coetaneously lit
by mirrored optical flaring
with mythic swans in the cells
with canicular bewitchment
of the southern suns
of angelic primevals
as dialectical dust of a primed immortal commingling
like the threshing of ice
like the burning of cataracts
rising like a flame
into the nonagons of living

Loss from Malediction & Exile

Across this Venusian leper screen
there is your memory
x-rayed in shark's gold
trying to forget the lungs
of your feverish cancellation
yet always wanting to monitor your teeth
with wild orational scalpels
as if I were taking account of neurotic polling germs
as if I had placed you at a level of dishonour
in order to disguise you
there has been nothing except surreptitious investment
the embrace of catalytic erosion & tartar

shadows
stultification
invisible carnivore's shale
invading my poisoned sage insomnia
seeking to canonize my absence
by means of tenebrous astral power
keeping myself preoccupied in blackness
yet your explosive sensual fructose
continues to inscrutably buffet
continues to pull me up by the throat
into a hallucinogenic sadness
into a demasted aria of brine
leaving me to rot
to exchange my convivial ferment for lice
for that hounded aristocracy of blankness
looking into harried effluvia for solace
for those energetic seizures
leaving me crossed
turned into a phoneme of rust
pledging myself to anathemas
to grotesque libidinal terror
without sunbolts
without seismic vertical sorcery
I remain tainted
squirming in a meadowlark furnace
committed to a cloud of erroneous calisthenics
dangerous
as olfactory ignition
breathing under fire logs
perspicaciously fumbling for dialectics to unscramble
eating a medley of tourniquets
doused in flickering urinal fire
trying to dissolve your harassments
your magnetic peacock harassments
your maniacal optical harassments
tortured
like a self-inflicted writhing
burning my faeces
expecting ice to explode

Breaking Through Linguistic Reason

The coded fog
of nude altimeters & hissing
as in the vortex of flaming tarantula ices
blowing up the lapses
in the scarcity of the trilingual memory
& so
the focus condenses
upon the explosion of gendarme folders
those weakened turquoise rivets
citing
in the grainery stalls
the motionless germs of elliptical contriteness
failing to structure
the bodily disappearance
of the arms & legs of spiders
therefore
the arcane spell
which makes the eyes stagger
which makes the blood fumes unite
into listless walnut incessance
extended into pagan archery sores
into jasmine & flaunting as connivance
floating across an alien zone
a rectangular turf
into bleached eclectic Seminole distortion
like a horizon flailing gunnery thorns
because each blatant dementia
procures owls as territorial
as pre-surface dawning enigmas
their monaural iguana majestics
their sonorous cooling
under curious sulphur tornadoes
their moth spillage
their equatorial burning dioxins
their microscopic seashell diverseness
because

the amperage
the arteries
must suffocate
the weird ecclesiastical pomposity of Christ
with their violet sails hoisted as scaly neutron dogs
into a trampoline of ciphers
like creeping soldiers' acidity
imaged as re-echoes to nothingness
to the facile codes of emptiness & habit
as in novels
romantically bellicose with motion
with despicable thoughts of action & reaction
as a claustrophobic rudeness
running on footskins & terror
generally braided with tedium
with the tortured marks of dense calendrical philosophy
therefore
there ceases to exist
my judgmental pallor
to chew
on bloodied cranial rinds
to scale at dawn
a greenish pelican aurora
because
it is the fish which haunts me
which takes me into alchemical ichthyosaurs' flagellation
into the glare of utter mortal disruption
along with mood swings
with meteors & cunning neon hysterics
now allowing me leave
to fly
to roam through the gulfs
through the blackened median kelp
through the shattered shores of smoking asteroid refinements

Toward the Endless Vertex Summit

I live
for the long-distance vertical empiric
for that eternity
for that rosebush aria
for that seamless chemical neutrality
for drafts of blind oxygen rhyming
to blow
on my arterial argonautica
yes
a moral pint of acid
nutrients
somnificantly heightened
by an infinity of claustrophobia
in a tunnel of grafted beeswax & urine

there is for me
the high plume of magic
the searing vertigo algaes
like a populace of incandescent photons roaming
the intergalactic wavelength vigils
the scaly neutron integers
magnetized
by anti-delusional boron & flailing

& each x-ray procedure
like a moving alloy
around a freshly born fireball munificence
within a pitch-black fortitude
coming to grips with itself
in an intensive orbit of telepathic tornadoes
the green meridians
the solitude
both vapour & horizon
the acidic dust
the shattered limestone galleys
hatching themselves

with nomadic igneous gulfs
with astral harlot wines
with antiphonal mental contusions
dropped away
into a swarming mass of pluperfect comets

as a gaseous veil of flying moulting stools
upon which
storms
& winds
& seasons
burning up the gastronomic poultice
with wind demon's surge
the ostrich
clawing its way out of hell
the burdensome transmuting
from a gazelle
from a hieroglyphic of sparks
like an ostracized
or climatic pseudo-pod
suddenly gold
with osprey hamlets
with surges of crystal mimicking
deadly broth & cider
into a piercing zone of Tsunamic cannibals' slivers
into a life skin
mealy
magnanimous
multitudinous
meandering

Astrobiology

Astrobiology—
an alien fluidics
subsumed in the aura

Desertion & Concealment

Camouflaged
under the bell of tubercular *nigredos*
under a storehouse of illiterate glazings
gawking at Carolingian blood nostalgia

camouflaged
by territorial bobbing
by seeming optical absurdity
by astral oxen stomping
across glowing irregular mud gardens
by ferocious jaguar plenums
by grainy fuel breaks in the blood

a sculpted sensory vacuum
an arcane x-ray hostility
full of mysterious horses
& transmuted galling wires

camouflaged in suspension

the race devoured
by stumbling
by breast burning
by neglectful neural rotations

an ornery leopard's vapour
subtracted & restored & maliciously multiplied
camouflaged
by a lack of riddles & overwrought eucharists & dung

camouflaged
ambiguously haunting texts
plagued by naked phosphorous & betrayal
holed up
thumbing pages of the Odyssey
poetically scribbling
an updraft of hawks in the margins

camouflaged
by protean fangs of cobra's velvet
by my desires coming up in aphid gusts
twisting under a perilous rock of lemmings
as I seek to read chartreuse into the opus of Kobo Abe & *
the Archpriest of Hita *

so I remain camouflaged
glare punctuating my fingers
the sun
like a solar emission of moray dust & piranhas
as I struggle with baroque palabras of Spanish
with Roger Bacon & the obscure fire of his *
powerful helical figments
with the seemingly lost Ahmose the 1st, *
with Queen Hatshepsut the Great *
with Akhenaton the "Great Reformer" *

camouflaged by seeming rigor
by spillage & seeming sodium denial
by scorching & herbivorous blindness
by utter verbal flotation & nothingness

because
a-Teutonic
listless
capable of large pounds of ennui

camouflaged
by dense verbatim drills
by subtractive in-palpitant anaemias
& so I stare
with freshly hatched thorium teeth
with melancholy dyspepsia
personally imprinted
on abstract magnesium mirages

my camouflage
lethal

Kaleidoscopic Omniscience

ambivalent
fractals
parabolas
methane laundries
copious under drill bits
& pressure

malachite prisms
& the stupendous sage
of loosened reptile moorings
me
damaged by attempted astronomical conquest
by hubristic parsec ventures
by acidically burning the replicated gums
of a hectically glimpsed galaxy on my forearm as a sign
burned
full of pantomime & dust screws
at my wits' end
looking for fragments
for impressive statistical taint
of seeming scholarly distance

you see
camouflaged as the burn king
as the partial prophet on the walls
of Minoan & hardened Iraqi magic

poisoned by the great thousand-year glimpses
into local galactic mesmerization
seeking bodily change
freshly kindled cellular transformation
wayward with strontium
with synapse &
alabaster boundaries

yes
camouflaged under the victory
of hot metacarpal alliance
blending live enchorial feathers

& marrows
& fractures
burning glottal stoppage
& utopias
"... contracting cells
placed at various depths of the skin ..."
yes
various moth chameleon
& electrical fragments

now a belt of circumpolar air
now a belt of quinine
& galvanic solfataras
under the breath
of a newborn plesiosaur's bleeding

camouflaged
with ancient Scythian chancres
Malthusian & nauseous
at the root cause
boiling in anathemas
corroded by Platonic fatigue

& so saliva
like incriminating camouflage technocracy
watering
the empty radix demons
the locust sands
the funerary muzzles
howling
seeking to magically sterilize
steaming glacial voids
a ballistical nerve war
camouflaged
as an emperor
as a shield of ruin & exile
as a somnific gunnery dial
as an oasis of witchcraft & stony
chariot polemics

Kaleidoscopic Omniscience

like a crow with unleashed
kryptonite & biting

camouflaged
drinking cups of scorching scorpion's wine
during an eerie December dusk
in the Madeiras
genetically linked as a lorikeet lizard
primeval
with flamingos & hunches
absolved
of wicked tourmaline lynchings

camouflaged
because I am a wizard
shivering
in my imaginary gemstone yurt
plagued by ponderous utilitarian suns

I have no image
no well-rounded vacuum
from which to call up my ghosts
my burning lecture units
sometimes there is the eastern seaboard
sometimes there is a drawl
sometimes Semitic scimitar slurrings
against the law
against the code of personal upkeep

camouflaged

spewed from the sac of an angel at birth
given the precarious Parish's incentives
to breathe

yes
a debacle of entrails &
incessant iridium hauntings
which has left me strange

which has left me with sudden codes
of occult chatter
because
with these numerator
with all these allopathic mirages
I remain
isolated
leaning on dazzled Sumerian inscription
stripped of worldly gold rush banners
beckoning
for Elysium comets
for smoking angels' cisterns

camouflaged
transfixed in my wavering
in my subtractive annealments
in my stormy Venusian ether & vestments
always fighting
dysfunctional grams of space
always in the throes
of disruptive mimetic networks
those crude lupercalian tigers
who seek to mount the bones
& connect the eyes with poison

tense with calcination & purges
camouflaged
fighting off
a learned commonness
concerned with a neurotic biblical 1st Kings *
with specific amalgams
from the classically chiselled soils of Coriolanus *

I opt
camouflaged
for mathematics & the tropics
mocking myself
with turpentine rinses
with tragic barracuda commitments

& so
camouflaged
emeraldine
the weather in my eyes always lunar with minerals
with storms across the iris
I remain skittish
static
with boron disjunction
a hardened subconscious largesse
floating across the waters
of a flaming Ligurian Sea

camouflaged
I proclaim myself the enriched
the implausible philosophical magnet
the alchemical ringworm antler
the incarcerated broach point

& so camouflaged
through these red distorting windows
through these multi-lineal bays
through analogical horse trots
finally
a multiplicand
flailing through horticultural mists
taking up
in my red & black fingers
a form of crab farming

a roughened progeny of blankness
camouflaged
saying to myself
scarecrows & gendarmes
pelted fumatory rums & forgetting
finally
hand written
cancelled in a gulf of rotating jasper & laundry
I gather my ironic sodium rumours
whispering

creeping along the scars
of precise
subliminal exposure

Bioluminal Self-Seeing

Snow eyes wafting
through volatile glycerin placebos
staring out
at triangular alien charismas
at marsh rabbits
centripetally spliced
by
flayed ozonal nerves
looking
always looking
for saffron blows
for bursts
for micrometer hinges
so as to chew on
insoluble terror
forcing
all glycerin placebos
farther & farther
into millet
the campfires hot
with pulmonic acid
with dog skin
with onyx & rapier urchins
to suddenly call on me
& have the moons turned around
in my flanks
to have all my wretched bohemias
brought up to the cranium
so that they glow
that they paradisically distribute

each longitudinal carcass
with teleology
with amniotic collisions
because
I have heavenly proof
that there is vertical depth
that there is hallucinatory honour
that there is a space where spasms exist
in which comets dissolve
throughout orbits of nothingness
because
to see time warp
into hot collusional craters
one must embrace
all the glazed baronial shatterings
the plutonic larval ivies
the sleepless anaemia of ravens
the terrified footing of Newtonian
quadrupeds
the burdensome glance of the frothing
mockery student
the treatise on fire with
ash point & extension
the blazing size of an
abalone colon
like a coronal sepia heritage
like the core
of levogyrational sorcery spinnings
like a star gone white
flaming out
in a suicidal opium tree

Clairvoyant Hummingbird's Braille

"Our glacial sunstroke love
in the pleasure of Peruvian exile

full of arrogance & incognito
full of brash copulation & whiplash

our aural burnings
like a sieve of edelweiss & liquor

sweating
an inchoate claw
a totemic moth
a beleaguered uplifted figurine of rubies
thereby gaining
our dominant hurricane bearings

our turquoise pyromania
as we grasp
macabre ecclesiastical drownings
bleak in its sundown causes
so as to sullenly smoke
like gazelles
or revolving crystal olives

it's as if I could freeze you
with all my boundless horse arts

my flame fingers
seeking to tangle their ivies
in the glistening rums of your magnetic fire belly

under a bordello of seashells
my mind intuitively quaking
like shamrocks
or a monster of eaten ionics
sliding across

salacious gemstone boundaries
breathing in my arms a magical citron

in the throes
of a green blast of primordial osteoblasts & tsunamis

an a-priori seething
like a magical iodine whippet
or chiselled marlin crossings
or Andean Hill Stars
flying around
the smoke of the sun"

Sumatran Mirror World

An eaten dictatorial bracelet wasting down to the natural bone rims, where the solvent touches glass, breaks into mirrors of greenish sunbeam disjunction, into the wrath of marauding cerulean tigers, the majestic mills, the fallopian rainbow winds, the crackling gemstone archery, the maniacal jaguar exposure, an explosive fictional code of disruptive rum braids, the ice gates, the agitational tropics, the shaking air equators, because I am building a palace of nerves, of harried sidelong gawking, of oblique crocodilian ensembles, of burning granary germs & piranhas, vinegar markings in high Sumatran mirror worlds, stoking the inseminated marginal fires, conjured within the epical breath of large mutational demons, for instance, the square root of masonry & arrows, the Einsteinian deeper beeswax memory wafting through a specialized mode of herbiferous millennia, over which winged terrapins crawl into the blackly moving modus of a star, tending themselves like bird bites, or transparent chariot haulers, I think of magnetic electrical broomsticks casting auras in which dolphins are made to believe in a foreign cannibal's rhetoric, like a stamp, or golden shackles on the arm, or choking magnetic shocks, magically strengthening the sun with intense heretical mirages, a clandestine lineage allowing me access to the other realms, those scale model freedoms of the infinite, those cherished horn blows of amnesia & wattage, covered in gnostic paradox I see the dialectical blood bones, the turquoise heavenly fractures, slitting carnivorous space/time, so you see I'm involved in exploring alchemical buffetings & nothingness, a haunted vertical nothingness, in which wizardry suddenly wells up into emancipated velvet, into blown dicta, into blinking sea tornadoes, into green prodromal meldings, because I invoke an empirical dizziness, a saturnine data of moody sapphire currents, replacing the torso & the eyes with ecstatic ultramarine convulsions, the view from Procyon & the Pleiades a brilliant motto of diamonds, the breath transfixed by arachnoidal pauses, & all moral invasion diminished to gas, & all miracles raised into nude bursts of ether, feeding from a crown of secretive skull bones & saffron

Within the Oracular Seahorse Mirror

Immersed
in this verdurous galaxy of salt
in this necrotic intaglio of wind
blown by the visual wheels of the abyss
I see the seahorse in this stormy optical dice
blinding the backs of shrewish winter eels
adding & subtracting its coffins
in this special floating foci mirror

with its pressures inveigled
like a holographic mescal
like a powerful Hottentot bionics
wavering at the core of a splendiferous practical amber

its images practicing drills
in a gigantic ambrosian leper field
gazing beyond a zone
of illusive inward metals
beyond a listless fertilization

blind
with dense gametophytes

it is like reading
with a smouldering interfixation
a treatise on locomotion
within the flames of a boldly coloured anti-sun
essential in its depths
in its risings
to its bony latticework of lightning
alighting
this spinning seahorse vacuum
"at right angles to the body"

it is one of the Syngnathidae *
with its dorsal fin in motion
with its "50 rectangular bony plates"
its occluded percentiles
ironically burning
at the peak of a minute ingestion

then the swarming from the masculine ventral pouch
of fiery newborn lanterns
of the fires of "50 species"
into new pre-fibular colonies
into wretched bodily wards of fire

because
in this crow-like speculum of nerves
there exists the power of an arcane heliotrope
of a virgin profanation
of a deep & protrusive transparency
so that
in its slow-motion movement
I see
in every fleck of carnivorous transparency
in every subaqueous star
the primeval rage
of an ocular underwater eagle

like a vertical rotation
like a flight of mineral in negative rococo
its elevations plunging downward
into dense barometers of squid
in the total waters of the sun
diffused
in a magic fumarole of rays
as a rhythm of squalls
in runic crystal optics
with vision translated
from a wild biology of corpses

the seahorse
with its primal rotating sugars
with its global turpentine advances
dissolving
& leaving the eye
in optical polarization
minus the mineralogy of the deluge
with its explosive facial chemistry
with its explosive facial compounds
preexisting in a gust of bells
living by visibility & lava

I see
"dissymmetry of molecular" combining
I see
blurred geometrical dalliance
electrically cancelled at the poles
of the "two types of crystals"
of "sodium ammonium nitrate"
with this fish horse of doubled rotations
seeking to refract
the quantum memory of osmosis
within the low inductive medium of the sea

in this mesmeric index by wave
by lethal ingestion by acid
the seahorse weaves its talons

within a rock of shaken nightmare phonemes
within the glance of diving bludgeoners' owls

so what I see
entangles the region
in an angular digestion of jewels
in a biogenic spiral of coral

because
the seahorse
with its turning kilowatts of zinc
with its slow-motion access to greater arcs & seizures
with its nutrients of flight linked to strange subduction prairies
stilled
in their first Precambrian volume
with the power of water
fused
in its magic Benguela current
in its Agulhas movement
blowing across Fuamoto Ridge
across the Atlantic-Indian basin
like a silent wolf
within a swarm of operas

the seahorse
in the virile state
of its haunted stationary resource
with its blending of coal & brightness
with its ammonia by diversity
it triggers litres in my system
in my enormous cyclical fury
cyclonic
with a passion
for declination & explosion

The Cryptographic Ocelot

To my friend the distant water owl Sulibika *

From this ravenous lectern of scars & anaemia, I greet you, with voracious glacial invectives, with heavenly avuncular muds, swarming like a nauseous cryptographic ballet, a spontaneous alkaline scorching full of wrathful classification & squab, I greet you with the antibiotic laser & russet sawtooth corsages, yes, the ice monsoons, the bottoms of criteria & stalling, yet, with all of this, there is auroral integrity, constant aural infinities able to hear the winding logomachic duration as it goes back to Venus, as it flies into solar pitch-blende burning, because here we speak of origin, of dissipated sun dust like flakes of asteroidal salmon flying up the turquoise balcony of light, into that hieratic moss, into that intuitive sodium garden, because I am a functioning mirage, a blanked cartography of raindrops, an asthmatic sorcery needle laterally riddling those Myrmidons mechanically emerging from the Saxon civil furnace, I am armed with the crucial invective, with the clipped tornado rejoinder, a mirage who squares his knights & his bishops within this cultural esplanade of panic, within this dizzying economic abradant, because I am the permanent heteroclite, the resistant heteroecious demon, who always carries in his eyes the glazed look of infinity, a tonic with mingled lightning persona, with the cycadaceous viral totemics, because I live within a boarded domain of psychic lunar vicinities I am forced to live by means of intensive verbal astonishment, I live by means of green beryllium adjustment, because you must admit that we are living amidst the ruins of broken dimensional timing, invaded by detritus from the more insidious realms, & so we, complete with angelic relation, are always camouflaged, are always like inscrutable bone patrols, like dramaturgic ions "... in the middle of action ...", in medias res, liminal, our faces contorted by those mercurial collisions with fissioning plutonic social dice, in this position of silence one is always accused of luminous errata, our charred emotional coatings, the loneliness of always confronting a stunted human vector burdened with insecticide & throbbing, staring at stagnant political falsity, at an occulted occidental opprobrium, at a dark miscarried confusion, at a heritage of butchery without surcease, during this poetic glimpse an empire falling to its knees, its economy staggered like a self-inflicted offal spilling over its soured Draconian taffeta, its blunted Germanic incisions, its tense participants shaking with palsy, with negative dialysis squarings, as for me, I have nothing to do with its addictive public notation, perhaps for me, being an anchorite in Notogaea, or in the Maldives, or in the Andaman Sea, certainly life has been silently arduous, a multiplication of injured mural roses, a chronic instinctual stinging, always under the tenacious fire of discomfort, each perspiration of the neural sacs, stung by a jagged demonology, by a collective hatred of crystal, so I greet you, the noiseless water owl full of territorial pincers, seeking out anomalous mists, flying from trees of neurological gold floating above a scalding summa of rice birds, you agree, one must schismatically sing, cryptically warping the magic vertical principle in order to probe with merciless transmissives into a simultaneous code of alchemical clarities, into an opening where the personality disappears like a trapezoidal voltage, & becomes Transylvanian, perplexing, like the ghostly state of Travancore, a phantom, a nonexistent treaty port, "a state of partial anaesthesia" full of lightness & burning, a loss of linear fatigue, yet always subject to wavering, to irradiated Jovian belts, we are those beings sucking secretive visional liquors, we are not beings seeking vivariums, simulations, vacuums of eternity in which certain jewels are grown, certain lights established, certain peacock seleniums impelled by superficial enrapturement, no, for us the impulsive breathing of transmuted zodiacs, of transfunctional ciphers & codes which set up folios lighted in the depths by an acrobatic jasmine star, a star which sucks in periodic lines of invisible amalgams, which refracts, which takes in particulars, which reverses & dialectically splits & creates a mood of invisible synecdoche, when in fact the ultimate mysterium is being given its breath, is being extended like an oblivious sun tree in its minor register, like a perpendicular wave climbing from a mysterious lunar box, I think of an arcane broach in which the same being appears split as in a dream, as in a neutral impersonal hearing field, because in this very instant I feel uplifted by this cryptic archaeology, by this deepened synonymous resurrection of oblique & universal anonymity, this deepened spirit of smoking sapphire & crystal, this anonymous haunt of hieroglyphic enigma, a code, now electrical, now wet, now burning with the power of an indecisive Mogul becoming magically translucent like a fine-tuned ostrich bladder given over to a higher coding magma, & yes, you hear me because I have no need to give myself over to a vocal spate of inferior translation, just as you expect from me incandescent frothing & obliterated mildew imbalance, as if I had hatched mercury in my groundswell wings, as if I had invented a voluminous & bombarded stellar uniqueness intent on erasing the quotidian linguistics of rubles & francs & deutschmarks & dollars, because as an ocelot, as an optical cat climbing sunbeam branches, I am never moored, never excited or destructive enough to suddenly give up my molten & take on the eyes of a treasonous herring, a herring which meanders through calculated rhubarb, never once advancing the tenets of a true strength of ice or of fire, never once confronting the dictatorial lamas of high religious illusion, never once will it act upon those gangrenous subplots keeping the ill-considered wheezings of history alive, to us, a battle for lost Elysium genetics at the root of this our injured parent galaxy, of this our home, our palace of fictive nightingale duties, as for the herring, it will always stay within the bounds of its treasonous smallness, it will always seek to divert by irritating mesmerization my relationship with water, to take away my ocelot wings, to take away my summas, my dense reflective explodents, as an ocelot I deal with the frictives of air & light, with the osteoblastical richness of hidden viridian havens behind the false imprisoning scowl of a diabolical deity, and so my friend, as a gift of perennial winter solstice I give you this hidden calico mirror which reflects those inner Sufistic phlogiston features, no matter that you are an owl, it reflects intensive solstice blendings, the potent cataclysms of paradise above your exploded character of longitudinal strain, I can say that I am permitted to live by means of a sulphuric axial grace, a spinning no more subject to burden, but with an exquisite musical depravity, allowing me to build those greenish rhinestone castles where colder Myrmidons are heated by brews of dialectical hymnals, by brews of heavenly heretical fuels, which become interior storm tree singing, eerie parallel chanting, & here, the actual virility of wisdom, of songs of cathartic neutron spirals, now, you can examine my throat for disclosure, take the temperature of my anomalous cadmium veins, watch the zone of my galactic silicate islands, because I am no longer the earth bearer, the illusional commander of a blinded water derby designed to keep in motion the hopes of a conventionally addled polis, never, because I have no deistical designs, no surreptitious uranium seizures thereby rationally attempting to explain a petty chalice of human crimes, be I weakened, or partially drunk with lingual blood, I will never become a pyroclastic constitutional imperator, full of imperatorial rules & pronouncements, from my secretive selvas I am a fiery radium expunger, a riverine Cagliostro, capable of gristle berries or smoking caviar russets, you see my friend, the human race exists annulled as a superluminal pornography, a human zone wasted in an ornament of haze & psychological destruction, a haze in which the sleight of hand dimension takes on the concrete draught of daily existence, full of corroded pantomime manoeuvres & juggling & God games, one must always build dazzling lacunae, false exterior puzzles, in order to feel the pulse of the seismic, the kindled horizontal morass where you & I constantly invade with ghostly stingray photinos, where you & I take on the daily weather of cosmic dram deletion, where we suffer from nucleic bites, from seeming angelic abandonment, where we continue to leap & fly although injured by tritons, and so, you see the cadence of my liminal trauma, my frank territorial marching pins, you see why I greet the fellow citizenry as MR. & MRS. OPTICAL DEGENERATE, as MR. & MRS. BLOODY CARNIVORE ARRAIGNMENT, they are a daily plutonic comedy indebted to delusion, to the microbes of self-deception, yet always failing to avoid the psychic tragedy of chewing on lesions, of always looking over their bland green shoulders for a neon herd of smouldering scorpions & vipers, they are as that seeing in a dream when an inevitable horse transpires blowing spurts of magma from its nostrils, inexorably intent on trampling their muscles into the earth, or feeling the wrath of huge destructor nails falling from an unknown lotus angle, they are frightened, & when they see us seeing them frightened with our grimace of reactive sundial poultice, with our pulled-back nostrils, with our dense observational butchery, they see we have no need to cling to one routine or the other, as for sentiment, let me call out the dog hackers, let me call out the messengers from cinematic snuff ballets, because I have no sympathy for beleaguerment, no sympathy for the pus-stained consumer's dollies, for mechanically approved rhetorical engagement, I've obliterated counting, I've seized a small gecko & like a piranha bitten out its belly, a solar-bellied cannibal piranha, so, there is no longer the need to wake up every dawn with a numerical memory of cultivated acquiescence always excusing the ladders of your dangling mental flesh, with faithless eruditions hounded between fireflies & granite, I could never be pleased as president on a pedestal of sickened holocaust phantoms sounding out splendiferous calls of my name, as for riches or insult, I have none, as for the shakti with the green hair & the golden fire in her fingers, she has yet to seismographically explode in my innards, she has yet to dash me against a bed of stone in suicidal copulation, no, she has not arrived, nor have her precursors been any more than lukewarm secular figments, any more than transacted failures morally superficial as relates to sacred corruption, to inspired Jezebelian honour, they will never find a milk brow in me, never a sustained diplomacy which negates the heritage of my pluperfect Olmec conjunction, yes, this is triumph, but in a sinister sense, like a broken eye, or a scaly citron flower, or an axe all covered with transliminal spiders

The Water Dog

> *The dog is the species most accustomed to accompanying early travellers by land and sea ...*
> —Thor Heyerdahl

Born under butane & water
under snapping fire of ice & razors
like a compass
pointed at the fact of combustible granite
pointing far beyond
the panorama of glaciers & icy landlocked schooners
to Antarctic labouring blisters
to special atmospheric codes
where ice sends up a smoke

like an exploded measuring jar
those expanded zodiacs of lightning

his tongue
crystal & fog & fire
his power
like a galaxy of anteater's rabies
a noxious weather vane of ions
pointing
Zambian kangaroo
the Isle of Wight
the beautiful moraines of Bermuda
pointing to the arcane solstice mountains
seeing like a cenobite
into the glassy fires of the Caspian Sea
into the blackened
imaginary grottos of the Sahara
a tense perilous compacting of weathers
in a unit of diamonds
cracked
on sandy Egyptian mountain ranges
filing its neurological hearing
so that the poles of Venus
connect
with the Gulf of Castellammare *
with the curving throat of Sicily
like a ruthless intentional steam

marking in the Mongolian steppes
with his hieroglyphical paws
of intuitive malachite & sunstroke
an Ibis in Genoa
a linseed spiral
part Damascus
part of the Swiss Thunersee & Paris

The grown dog amounts
the magical snout alignments
gazing

at threads of Amazonian lice
at its headwaters rotting
pointing
kabbalistically to its bottoms with his breath
pointing
to the asteroidal fields of Ceres
the darkened pre-globular entropies
mesmerized
with howling & starlight
with magic geometries of panic
a diviner
analogous with landscapes of darkness
briefly dazzled
by twilight & pumice
who seizes every particle of ground

his breath pointing
to butchery shelters & loneliness
like a telepathic pine juice
seething
microbiology & vineyards
howling
at those sacred iguana dawns
looking for the magical cracks in the skin of space
sucking in eclipse & lightness

the principal force of ice balloons
a wave of lotus junctures

all the sundown bluing
all the nucleic borium breathing
across the asteroidal isles
across the proton-neutron
of this life
of this present profusion
the force
of bays & winds & stars
the deep mercator blankness
the mutant compass slavings

the anti-osmium susurrations
issuing from his electrical skull
from the musical stride of his forceps' blackness

because of his fierce navigator's bondage
Asiatic
etheric
his wayward nitrogen calendar
his stupendous rose war ignitions
because
he is the water dog
the dog
between non-being being & being
able to distinguish the flux
between Graham Bell Island
& the Bay of Biscay
between
Revillagigedo in the Mexican Pacific
& the inland flames of Ulan-Bator

the dog angel
at the origin of hydrography & fire
at the genesis of arc-light & magnesium

the dog angel
the water dog on fire
the synonymous Arctic star
the occult illuminal wire
smelling
the blood
the spaces
the cunning ammonia
of cyclic ambrosial dimensions

A National Day in Bangladesh

Absorbed
up to the heart bone
in ferocious glacial mosquitoes
under boats of larvae
& transfixed minimal dust
Bangladesh
like water in the throat
of your tenacious malarial hedges
like rotted tombstone vapours floating
in the muscles
& every ligature absorbed by panic
by dislocation & seizure
by birth
with its sickened dodecandrian calendrics
with its insidious dry-dock implosions
setting sail
upon a voyage of impetigo & rashes
the bullocks plagued
with scales & amoeba
with sudden fish diseases
like soil
monstrously trickling from the womb
like bread on fire
with colourful hummingbirds' trichinosis
the diet
a swimming Moray hen
a platter of Vultures
with hemlock
with hallucinogens scattered inside your protein cadavers
with paint chipped off your teeth
with your national swans defrocked
by your growing monetary vomit
with procedures
which cause
the moon to leak neurosis
which causes

the brain to send up its neurons
to make the chaos swell
into a paradoxical amber
frying
an improper lesion
sprayed
with a Gordian argot
with a flame of black lanterns & ice
with the shadow of swinish children's diseases
this is life
this is the sundown moat
which finds its face
unlocking cannibals' barriers
like a cow
feeding itself to death on parasites & dolphins' blood
mimicking marrow
seizing in its mental rods
broken turquoise stains
their arbitrary baking
their monstrous nomadic ions
flushed from paradisic eternity
and so Bangladesh
you squint
into dead brown letters of the flag
into individual bloatedness
and see the capricious jaundice
of negative divinity
like an immobilized eaglet strangling on moon rash
saturated
with preconditioned soots & barleys
with a stony armament of wheezing tubercular markings
the spots
rolling from your naked skin like rancid
plutonium dice
like carrier pigeons
assaulted in the doorway of banishment
with a sign upon the portal
reading
"PRIMARY SULPHURS CULLED FOR DISRUPTIVE ANAEMIA"

and so Bangladesh
the burden falls
obliquely into the hands
of your leaders who launder their psyches
with gizzards
with the sky inverted
to make toolmaking poisons
on this day Bangladesh
you are slated to become a nonexistent artery
a nonequatable slattern
lost in irreparable jargon
this is the rope
peopled with drill bits
with Pompeiian migratory saunas
with a sullen oblivious wool
because
the peacock is your home
is a Seminole chariot
blown out through the holes of a faulty
nicotine destructor
so this is my prayer
that you wake up the asteroids
that you pillage from the ethers
the raw designs of political erasure
to disregard your linear scrambling
purged of those imperial manacles of death
taking on the fire
of a luminous deadliness
an atonal wind bell
like a spectacular waterfall across
the spectrum of the voiceless Trojan Planets
because
I say
Bangladesh
you must resurrect tornadoes on Mars
you must clean the face
of bluish cadmium mirrors
becoming
a flotational scarlet

around the angry planetary edicts of Vega
on this day Bangladesh
you will leave earth
as if impregnating a woman
by the mouth with saliva
there are the miracles of Neptune
Carina
Dorado
chewing on magical x-ray ascension
getting up
from your bed of suicide
& flying

Anti Euro-Psychosis

Poised against sensations
of Eurocentric embellishment

poised against its drift
against its cruel episodic misnomers
in order to see my life
as mirrored Coptic uranium
as bluish desert somnifics
in a wave of wordless archery candles

me
poised against its squalor
as a nerve curving in flightless sorcery dungeons
singeing from the sky
a green line of stars
slashing with my wings
its zoneless parabolas
its technological plutonics

poised
as if seething between haunted rabies & drachmas

or
the war between turmoil & suddenly blended amnesias
then the seductive cannibal orations
kindled by curious asphalt & Persia
poised against
Eurocentric chastisements

yes
swans
in the bell throwers' wavelengths
barking
like a scab or a heartache
like a floating tumbleweed mirror
like a hungry sand dune clock
or a homunculus
spread
across an ashen galactic portrait of fire

how much sun can I take?
how much abuse from eroded mental cathartics?

here I am
mocking the current human catatonia
mocking the race
as it sails suspended
meandering through lustrums

a waking marginal burst
as if under the wound of ravens' bread
as if I had swallowed
a pictographic skull of burden & slavery
& had emerged
from a merciless syntactical folly
with heightened synovial dressings
with a graft of transparent skeletal arthritics
poised
like blind uranian combustion
discarded & ruthlessly savoured as a sigil

therefore
a blank memorial tower
dismissing the xanthochroids
with their blood counts
their molecules
their poisons
their folly

Modernity

In the West
cold vulgarity by quanta
a mecca of training
of blinded anchoring bellows
sweating beneath the flow
of poisonous cortical ink

the person then exists
like incinerated lightning
like a code of indifferent reptile plasmas

the eyes become melded with narcotic plains
with a range of mutilated ores
where the brain stem founders
by placing a mirror in one's anachronistic moats

bread then condenses
breeding on tragic lepers' standards
breeding on tragic lepers' incidentals

parenthetical
interjacent
in a deadening anti-resonance campaign
with the voice obliquely roaring in the purity of irregular greyness

the empire with its sun
& classic clause of abbreviation
like a commonplace novena
in a labouring dragon's fang prognostic
across
an in-irradiated gulf
measured by the ciphers of shapeless fumatory limbs

Bridge as Poisonous Anti-Harvest

Not the archaic link
nor the primeval span
which solders smoke with necessitous smoke

but a girder of blind monerans
hoisted from a strange tumultuous repercussion of sclerotics
spanning the silt of covetous dyestuffs
of cold political oceanics
being suspension as poisonous anti-harvest
conveying Myrmidons of deadened vagabond procession
across its sleet of objective zeal
not
as a talismanic span
or flattened stones thrown across waters
but that which connects perception with perception

the bridge of internal rainbows
dismissed
& charged as the compacted dust of a postmortem heron

I think of the modern bridge
as praise for a dazed vehicular zone
to a zealous zodiacal ambit
where electrons fuse in a velocity of hubris
like a furious electrical salt
with its cables

with its illusionistic braces
administrating rust
administrating vermin
voracious in its lineage
like an oath advanced against slaughtered Cherokee nations
& the workers in this repetitive ozone
consumed in nettling microdots
in feral blistering moats
above the mined ballistics of the sea

the actual corpse of the bridge
built in timber caissons
compressed air-pressured caissons
hoisting a bloodied diamond
a brutish melancholia by graft
as if the mind were composed of exasperated roughage
in which sunbeams default by means of toxic carrion trains
inverted diesel mules
iniquitous stoic models
in which beings are suppressed
by hammers
by drills
by worlds which produce the eaten rhythm of blood

& so the pulleys
the stanchions
emitting a rufescent wool of panic
no longer the ideal of machinery
no longer the seminal force of mechanistic repose

what exists
is the movement of vain a-rapturous troglodytes
across a Stygian mural of marble
across crude & obsessive measuring germs
where the magic is obscured
within this land of wasteful miracle & cure
within this land of the despicable daily wage as bondage
making promissory notes within the mockery of scandal

& what lives in my ire
is not only the bridge of Brooklyn
but "the Tavanasa ... over the Rhine in Switzerland"
or the "Pont Albert Louppe" measured over zones in Brittany
of the monstrous Humber near Hull in England

such life
marked by Freyssinet's "concrete" "compression" *
by its piercing wires
by its forced illusional spoilage
announced
in corrosive ¾ weight
its temper a void
an electrical vibrating distance
being nothing more than a sluice into vacancy
a listless form in mirage

Albania & the Death of Enver Hoxha

Sacrifice
closely paralleled with sadness
with darkened lunar wounds in the brain
the thoughts laced with paralysis ciphers
the voice full of fumaroles & muffled x-ray voltage
the cells cold with exhaustive inversion

& so
all pronouncements become tautological
derisive
each attempt at revival sundered with
a wearied dysfunctional torment
with psychic nuclear crippling &
hyperborean chills
all attempts at recovery pushed back into limbo

if one could look at the soul
it would take on the grief of a savagely splintered darkness
a simile of cacti & arrowheads
burrowing into the crucially exposed eyestalks of crustaceans
the face always stained by a ruthless sabulosity
coupled by paranoia & blasting

the expiring Enver Hoxha *
prone
like a skull on a slab of Marxist invectives
with a glut of crushed worms slipping from his forehead
lying there
with personal rabies on the breath
an ignited grandeur
coming out in riddles of oracular demon pulleys
rust burns smoking below the stones of his flesh
his dictatorial mutterings
like a spurt of unseasonable frog gills
like a grotesque insecticidal frenzy calling out
from tormented histamine gardens
calling out from decrepit Dodonas
diseased with insidious miosis

Hoxha
with secretive bone grafts
with rational murdering solutions
always hardened
like blackened myasthenias

all his rebellious hirelings
slaughtered in a square by machine gun & mortar
the killers surreptitiously empowered
by mutative alienation
by a heart of stunted mangrove blisters
& his dreams
like a definition of mustard gas
"irritating, blistering … disabling …"

Hoxha
sucking in fumes from his after-death exposure
his astral obliteration
like an exquisite brew of heinous polonium cocktails
full of disintegrated polyhymnials
full of mental pollution & polymorphic pariahs & sweating
full of stunted radium volcanoes & the sociology of crows

in his Stygian neurosis
this demon
atop asphyxiation & thrones
always remains demasted
in haunted wallowing aspersions of asynchronous assuagement
his lost Malpighian body
directing his troops across a coldly burning land
with all the embraceable contusions of a stifling necrology

"… report to his majesty
that the bones have been crushed
that the spleens are now rotted
that all is in order"

the sun
like an Albanian nothingness
like an exposed nerve of singing suddenly turned over
into neutralized materia & banished
as a dried pineal concentration

& here we have Enver Hoxha on his deathbed
breathing in parasites & noxious Arabian vesications
breathing in malodorous turbellarian rains
the remaining pores of his body filled with a furious
obturation
with a dense clinical stoppage
taking a poll of his highly conducive death counts
his obverse vivisectionist commandments
the population:
an arrested quotient
a blank but undivided numerical dogma

wrestling with desires in moulded sparring chambers
burning in Stalinist dialectical hells

& so Hoxha
with his convinced in-solutional ravings
speaking out
with his oily wolverine's tongue
wrapped in his popular grave clothes of blackness

there were days
when the moon began to howl at high noon
when all the aromas were suspended
when all the corpses were dredged up & eaten
when each anniversary of living
was marked by insidious facial scarring
by vicious dog bites on the buttocks

this was reason
& so the populace
full of carcinoma & rugas
their eyes cast down into sacerdotal infernos
into cold intensive lesion mining
could only witness their faces in puddles of urine
could only imagine how a morning of restive balneology would feel
how a life of campanology could brighten the darkness

but always disaster
grey
& permitted to burn like a daily burden of
calcinated litmus
like a corpse with a vertebra of flukes
tossed up from the Adriatic shallows
tossed up in its ashen lonely demeanour
as an isolated cargo of worms

& Hoxha quoting remnants of Engels
concerning "motion" & "divisibility"
"kinetics & bodies"
under his spartan flag of pickaxe & rifle

the horseless carriage banned
the blood supply diminished
the "hillsides
a jagged line of misty peaks"
like horizontal shards like "gigantic" electrocardiograms
more occluded than Tibet
creeping along "the Boulevard of Fallen Heroes"
where one can feel the peasants feeding on grasses
seeking to mobilize their anomalous wrath to production
the cities full of "windowless walls" &
a "heritage … of blood feuds"
yes Albania
like a "black double-headed eagle" on a
coursing field of blood
its exteriorized sacrifice ministries
its ferocious injury battalions
its cold atheistic medallions charged with a-charisma & spite
like a premise or a scar
or a pure line of rote from its suppurating memory
its "mosques" turned into "stables"
comets & asteroids banished from the language
& so
one is given "mechanics"
the "interchange of motion & equilibrium"
& the "measurable transference of motion"
the "quantitative expression"
the hatred of "alien morality"

& Hoxha
purged of all animal sentiment
his deathbed
like a broken imperial rock
seething with a secretive personal dissension

even the "Directorate of Agitation" is crumbling in his vistas
because he smells
the insurrectional molecules of the infinite
blowing into his itinerate pantomime chamber
the inscrutable Hadean depths

Kaleidoscopic Omniscience

a group of denuded chromium puppets floating
before his eyes
his bizarre self palpable plainness
thrown into the face of cosmic betrayal
ulcerations & demons appear beside his visage
even his own skull appears on the plainly coloured revetment

& the sun
once simply a mechanical furnace
is now a thrust of light
burning up his bones
& the bulging knot of old "foxtrots"
& purges

Glossary

Asia

Coupled monkey & demon: Tibetans "claim as their first parent a monkey which crossed the Himalayas and there married a she-devil of the mountains."

Bon religion: Pre-Buddhist, indigenous to Tibet, its "black hatted" priests were exorcists of demons.

Nāgārjuna: Born "four hundred years after Buddha's death," he upheld the "Buddha's deepest teaching." His Five Collections of Reasonings established "emptiness as the mode of existence of all phenomena," thereby burning "the fuel of bad views" and clearing "away mental darkness."

Tsepon Shakabpa: "Tibet's Finance Minister" at the time of the Chinese invasion.

Sera: The "great Sera Monastery, a focal point of anti-Chinese feeling, four miles outside of Lhasa."

Khambas: Fierce independent tribesmen in Eastern Tibet.

Tsamba: A Tibetan staple of "parched barley meal ... kneaded with water into a doughy paste," with a "pinch" of "brackish" "salt," its mass being "eaten uncooked."

Srongtsan Gompa: First Tibetan king, flourished during the middle of the 7th century.

Karakorum: 13th century Mongol court where Tibetan lamas were acknowledged.

Tsong-khapa: 15th century lama from "north-eastern Tibet" who reformed the earlier Buddhist mode, establishing an unwavering celibacy in the monasteries' confines, and purging an active demonology. Started the "Yellow Cap sect."

Altun Khan: A "western Mongol" potentate who conferred on "the most important Lama in Lhasa" at the time the title of "Vadira Dali Lama," the first use of "Dalai" "meaning ocean and so boundless." The year – 1576.

17 Point Agreement: Forced agreement signed by a "five man group of Tibetans" without authority, "sealed by them with a seal forged by the Communists ..."

Loka: Khamba enclave south of the Tsangpo River.

Rinehen Dolma Taring: "... an educated Tibetan woman who followed the Dalai Lama into exile in India" during the Chinese bombardment of Norbu Lingka, March 17th 1959.

Padma Sambhava: "The Founder of Lamaism."

Vasubandhu: Buddhist logician from India. 4th century A.D.

Dignaga: Pupil of Vasubandu.

Dharmakīrti: Buddhist logician from India. 7th century A.D.

Euleuth Tartars: Sacked Lhasa in 1710, and hailed from the locale of Jungaria, between the "highlands of Mongolia and the lowlands of Turkestan."

Kingku Dut'ang, Gewa Dut'ang, Chensi, Kingku Dhuni, Shāchan Dhuni, Shalu, Chuba, Pet'ang Gyeba: All Tibetan teas, the central drink of Tibet.

Chumbi Valley: Between the borders of Sikkim and Bhutan. 9,780 feet in elevation.

Armasa: armas – Latin for arms; *sa* – suffix, meaning "small arms."

Yamdok Lake: "... a vast inland sea without outlet." It is 14,900 feet above sea level. In Tibet.

Sivok: A gorge in Sikkim called "Cleft of the Winds," 500 feet above sea level.

Tarkhola: "... stifling clearance in the forest ..." 900 feet above sea level. Also in Sikkim.

Devendrabuddhi: Pupil of Dharmakīrti whose mind was focused at the level of "direct meaning." Called by Prajnākara Gupta "a fool."

The Cashmere School: Saw the Buddha as "a metaphysical entity," and was founded by Dharmottara around 800 A.D.

Sa-skya-pandita: Composed the "classical Tibetan logical work of 18th century A.D. A short treatise in mnemonic verse."

Rendapa-Zhonnu-lodoi: Teacher of Tsong-khapa and the "author of an independent work on the general tendency of Dignāga's system." Lived 1349-1412 A.D.

Nyāya: Indian school of thought which crossed swords with Buddhist logicians between the 6th and 10th century A.D. It posited "realistic epistemology."

Kamba Pass: 16,500 feet above sea level. The "last of all the passes on the road to Lhasa ..."

Tsangpo Valley: Located in Central Tibet, 12,100 feet above sea level.

Lord & White-horned Lady: They close the upper end of the Tsangpo Valley, each rising to 20,000 feet in height.

Garhwal Himalayas: In North-West Nepal at the border of Tibet. 22,907 feet in height.

Changt'ang plateau: "lofty desert tableland" "above Lhasa" "unfit for human settlement..."

Navamsa: In Hindu astrology it means essence of the soul. It is the 9th harmonic. Pronounced *na-vam-sha*.

Year of the "Iron Tiger": October 7th, 1950: Chinese invasion into Eastern Tibet.

Tsetang: "Chinese garrison" annihilated by Tibetans towards the close of 1958.

Norbu Lingka: Home of the Dalai Lama attacked by Chinese forces on March 17th 1959. The Dalai Lama was forced to flee to India. Its locale, Lhasa.

Muru: Monastery famous for its teaching of the occult and "Black Magic." In the "north-east corner of Lhasa."

Glossary

Nächung: A leading oracle in Lhasa.

Eight Lucky Signs/Glorious Emblems: "... which are figured on Buddha's footprints, and embroidered and painted on innumerable articles and furniture ..." They are: 1. "The Victorious Wheel of an empire on which the sun never sets; 2. The Lucky Diagram called by the Tibetans Buddha's entrails...; 3. The Lotus Flower of heavenly birth; 4. The Vase of divine ambrosia of immortal life; 5. The two Golden Fish of good fortune, the mascots of Yamdok Lake; 6. The White Umbrella of Sovereignty; 7. The Conch-shell trumpet of Victory; 8. The Victorious Banner."

Gyges: King of Lydia (687-652 B.C.)

Croesus: King of Lydia (56 1-546 B.C.)

Haiti

Songhai & Mali: "... powerful medieval states in West Africa..."

Tontons: Formed in 1958 by François Duvalier as protection against political and civil unrest, prompted by the attempted invasion of "ex-Captain Alix ... Pasquet" in July of 1958. Recruited from the lower classes, they were known for their incessant brutality. They were formally known as the Tonton Macoutes.

Long curved machetes: Used by Macoutes; "known as coulines ..."

Avenue John Paull II and Rue Martin Luther King: Streets along which angered Macoutes ferociously marched November 29th 1987 in opposition to free elections.

Mackandal: "African-born leader" in Haiti who commanded his followers to poison "their white oppressors, serving up death in broth and tea and juices, ladling it into wells, mixing it into medicine."

Petro: New world voudou, formed from the rage "which the African suffered" as a result of unprecedented "brutality" and "displacement."

Yaws: A crippling tropical disease affecting three-quarters of all Haitians. Highly contagious, "it enters the body in the form of a spirochete through the soles of the feet. ... it eats away at its victims. Their limbs wither and deform, they suffer great purulent ulcerations all over their bodies, and they lose noses and lips just as lepers do."

Luckner Cambronne: François' "bagman" and "Simone's lover." Owned "blood-plasma business" which "shipped five tons of plasma a month to American laboratories directed by Armour Pharmaceutical, Cutter Laboratories, Dow Chemical ... "

François and Simone: The dreaded Duvaliers, holding power as a couple from 1957 to April 21st 1971, the latter date being the death of François.

Yvonne Rimpel: "... a feminist leader" who had dared to criticize Duvalier concerning the colours of the "national flag." Raped. Left for dead. Resumed her life in terrified silence.

Bel-Air: "... oldest neighbourhood in Port-au-Prince, and one of its poorest and most crowded. After Duvalier became president" it was a "hotbed of opposition."

Faustina: Wife of Marcus Aurelius, known for "gross profligacy." Said to be the consort of gladiators.

Maturin and Walpole: Charles Robert Maturin, "Irish writer of Gothic fiction, author of *Melmoth the Wanderer*. Called by Lautréamont, 'The Godfather-of-Shadows.'" Horace Walpole, "English statesman and wit." "Author of the first Gothic novel, *The Castle of Otrano*."

Harold Courlander: "American ethnomusicologist" who studied and collected Haitian music for years. Known for his classic book, *Haiti Sings*, written in 1939. An old acquaintance of Duvalier, he was invited to the latter's "political headquarters" to discuss larger housing for the "Bureau of Ethnology" and was greeted by a bizarre scene of Duvalier, "at the centre of a long table," in a "pitch-dark room" lit by "dozens of candles," surrounded by Macoutes, who all wore dark glasses. The year, 1958, Duvalier's first as newly installed leader.

Cowering cook: In *The Satyricon* the cook is forcibly stripped by order of the tyrannical Trimalchio for failing to gut a pig.

Fidel Castro: When Fulgencio Batista was overthrown "Duvalier panicked" and "wooed Castro like a desperate lover" sending to Cuba "gifts of medicine" and pardoning "several important political prisoners."

Tortuga, Matheux mountains, city of Jérémie, Port Salut: Geographical locales of Haiti.

Damballah Oueddo: "place name related to the *loa* brought from the Dahomean seaport of Whydah." The name intones a special quality of benevolence, respected authority, and prestige.

Baron Samedi: "Lord of the Cemetery, of the crossroads," "whose ... best-known expression is the zombie." "Petro equivalent of Legba."

Dahomean Rada: "The Rada rites" "stand" "for the basic African tradition" of "stability" and "integration."

Signorelli's 'Condemned': "Italian painter, the most powerful exponent of the nude before Michelangelo ..... "The Condemned In Hell" is one of his "frescos in the chapel of S. Brizio, Orvieto Italy."

Eric Brièrre: A "young mulatto who tried to assassinate Duvalier" ... "tortured to death in Fort Dimanche while his father had to listen from another cell."

Yvan Laracque: A rebel invader who was killed and had "his fly-infested corpse propped into a garden chair at a major downtown intersection."

Sanette Balmir: A "convicted thief and lesbian," she was appointed by Duvalier as "commandant of Jérémie's Macoutes," known for her ferocity.

Gehenna: "a place of torment and burning."

She-devil/lower mesopelagic: The she-devil is found at depths of 10,000 feet. It is luminous, monstrous, and degenerates the male, only using it for sperm, as *the latter attaches itself to the female at maturity. The lower mesopelagic is the "twilight" realm at ocean depths between 1,600 and 3,300 feet.

Omosudis lowei: "... predacious fish" "of the hammerjaw family" possessed of a "powerful bite." Lives "at depths" from 660 to 3,300 feet.

Fort Dimanche: On the "outskirts" of Port-au-Prince, "the death site of thousands of Haitians."

Croatian Ustashi: "During the Second World War," it was an arm of the SS who amazed their progenitors by burning their victims alive.

Gulf of Gonâve: Gulf northwest of Port-au-Prince.

Lucetie Lafontant: Wife of Jean-Jacques Dessalines Ambroise, "a founding member of the Communist Popular Party of National Liberation. Tortured to death while still pregnant."

Jumelle: Former political rival whose swollen corpse was stolen and delivered to the palace where Duvalier (in the presence of Macoutes) "mounted the body and called upon its spirit."

Trou Foban: Cave in the Haitian mountains where Duvalier coaxed its evil spirits to return with him to Port-au-Prince.

Abel Jérome: Barracks Commandant during Vespers of Jérémie, 1964.

Sansaricq family: Mulatto family murdered in the Vespers of August 1964. Duvalier monstrously sent a wire to save the family after he knew they had been murdered.

Catechism and Breviary: In *Catechism of a Revolution*, Duvalier proclaimed himself the equal of the nation's founders. His *Breviary of a Revolution* marked the ten year anniversary of his power, which copied "Chairman Mao's Little Red Book."

Ghede: "... master of the abyss into which the sun descends." "... the night Sun, the life which is eternally present, even in darkness."

Govi: A clay jar in which the soul is contained after death.

Cordillera Central: Haitian mountains.

Haitian Massif du Nord: Haitian mountains.

Rada voudou: Old world Dahomean voudou more concerned with beauty than with rage.

Harmolodia: Coined word. Imagined instrument of harmony.

Ignatics: Plural of the coined word, ignatic, which means mirage or phasma of fire.

Erzulie-Ge-Rouge: Ferocious Petro Goddess of passion and promiscuity.

Vevers: "Symbolic caballa-like designs drawn on the ground to invoke the *loa* at ceremonies, made of wheat or maize flour or ashes."

loas: Dieties of Haiti.

Sources consulted for Asia:

Meditation on Emptiness, Jeffrey Hopkins
Buddhist Logic, Volume One, Th. Stcherbatsky
Lhasa & Its Mysteries, L. Austine Waddell
A Literary & Historical Atlas of Asia, J.G. Bartholomew
Genocide In Tibet A Study In Communist Aggression, Edited by Rodney Gilbert
Trespassers On The Roof Of The World, Peter Hopkirk

Sources consulted for Haiti:

Divine Horsemen: The Living Gods of Haiti, Maya Deren
Haiti, Elizabelh Abbott

Stratospheric Canticles

Mandean utopias: "Every being in the physical universe has its counterpart in the heavenly Earth of Mshunia Kusta, inhabited by the descendants of a mystical Adam and Eve."

Navanax: a marine mollusc closely related to the sea hares. Large (up to 12 centimetres) "and strikingly coloured with many yellow dots or lines, and a number of blue ones on a brown background. It is a voracious feeder on other opisthobranchs, which it tracks down by following their mucous trails. Overtaken prey are engulfed whole by a sucking action of the pharynx. Its large egg masses may contain 800,000 eggs."

Enoch: solar hero. "His years are numbered at 365."

Bardo: the state between death and rebirth.

Chandas: "The Vedic idea that the Spirit of creation framed all the movements of the world ... in certain fixed rhythms of the formative word, and it is because they are faithful to the cosmic metres that the basic world-movements unchangingly endure."

Alewahs: coined term, meaning "bitter cry" (*ale,* bitter; *wah,* cry).

Ramses: reigned at Thebes 1,300 years before Christ.

Hatshepsut: One of the most famous of the Egyptian Female Pharaohs who ruled in the 18th dynasty. A line of female rulers which extends from Nitocris in the 6th dynasty to Cleopatra in 30 B.C.

Akhenaton: Egyptian pharaoh, ruled circa 1350 B.C. Called the Heretic King. "Thirteen hundred years before Christ he preached and lived a gospel of perfect love, brotherhood, and truth. Two thousand years before Mohammed he taught the doctrine of the One God. Three thousand years before Darwin, he sensed the unity that runs through all *living* things."

Alloestrophas: coined from the word "Alloestropha." A term used by Milton in the Preface to *Samson Agonistes* to describe verse composed in stanza (or strophes) of irregular length and construction.

Glossary

Gersoppa: waterfall in India (height: 830 feet).

Kalambo: waterfall in Zambia (height: 786 feet).

Middle Cascade: waterfall in California (height: 910 feet).

Peace: North American river; empties into Slave River.

Don: European river; empties into the Sea of Azov.

Snake: North American river; empties into the Columbia River.

Wood meal: a gelatine dynamite.

Aluminium powder: mixed with ammonium nitrate, it is an industrial explosive.

Dynobel: an explosive for use in coal-mines.

Aconcagua: volcano in the Andes of Argentina (height: 23,080 feet).

Cotopaxi: volcano in Ecuador (height: 19,498 feet).

Karisimbi: volcano in the Congo (height: 14,787 feet).

Lepton circus: a group of subatomic particles which do not take part in strong interactions. The group includes electrons.

"Imago Ignota": "characterized by the quest for the obscure as a self-sufficient goal, and by the representation of 'harmonious wholes' whose fascination lies in their remoteness." '

Proxima Centauri: the star nearest to the Earth (other than the Sun); it is the coolest, reddest member of the triple star system Alpha Centauri, approximately four light years away.

Procyon: a double star system approximately 12 light years away.

Sirius: a double star system comprised of Sirius A, twenty-three times brighter than the Sun, and its dwarf companion Sirius B, the latter discovered by the Dogon without the aid of a telescope.

Groombridge: reference to a double star system, about eight light years away, catalogued by the English astronomer Stephen Groombridge (1755-1832).

Eridanus: in the constellation Eridanus, there exists a cool red triple star system, about sixteen light years away.

Sohravardi: flourished in northwestern Iran and "carried out the great project of reviving the wisdom or theosophy of ancient pre-Islamic Zoroastrian Iran; he set the seal on this achievement by dying as a martyr in Aleppo in the fullness of his youth, victim of the vindictiveness of the "doctors of the Law." Died in the year 1191.

Najm Kobra: guided the Sufism of Central Asia toward the practice of meditation with particular attention to the phenomena of light, especially chromatic succession punctuated by the significance and preeminence of green light.

Kaleidoscopic Omniscience

Crepusculum vespertinum, crepusculum matutinum: a twofold twilight, the former no longer day but not yet night, the latter no longer night but not yet day. This seems to define the liminal nature of being human.

"Emerald Rock" of "Hermes": The "heavenly pole," where beings are seen in the "light of the angel." Hermes, in his ascent to the celestial pole, is the hero of "eschatological ecstasy."

Galapagos Hawk, Japanese Crested Ibis. Arabian Ostrich, Barabary Stag, New Zealand Bush Wren, Key Largo Wood Rat: all members of extinction.

Oort clouds: clouds of comets which surround the solar system, discovered by the Dutch astronomer Jan Oort.

Fornax system: a cluster of galaxies in the constellation Fornax.

Draco complex: a cluster of galaxies in the constellation Draco.

Andromedan wave: reference to the large neighbouring galaxy, also known as M31, two and a half million light years distant.

Yaka: a Congolese community which uses masks in initiation rites. The masks are "made of rough bush materials and have relatively abstract features."

Fulani: a Sudanese community whose art is "mostly nonrepresentational, their leatherwork decorated with geometric appliqué."

Congolese nauga: a harp fashioned from a hollow log over which a skin membrane is stretched. "Plucking the strings produces music with an unusual buzzing tone."

Cantabrian: pertaining to the Cantabri, "an ancient warlike people of northern Spain."

Timur: Mongol conqueror of the fourteenth century who "altered the political complexion of western Asia. In his capital of Samarkand, there came into favour, in addition to book illustration, ink sketches on separate sheets, usually highlighted in gold, through the stimulus of the Far Eastern example."

Behzād of Herat: the greatest master of Persian painting. "Behzād understood how, even in his most populous compositions, to differentiate every single figure in countenance and bearing; his palette was extraordinarily rich, especially in warm, full tones, and this enabled him to individualize his portraits by the employment of numerous colour-nuances for costumes and even for flesh."

Harmolodium: coined word, from the Greek *harmos,* "a fitting," and *alodium,* "a full and free possession." In short, harmony as freedom.

Impulse & Nothingness

Isidorus the Younger: Architect during the time of Justinian who rebuilt the dome of the Hagia Sophia after its destruction by earthquake in 553 A.D.

Darlingtonias: A genus of snakes in the *Colubridae* family.

Glossary

John Cade: Leader of popular revolt during the reign of Henry VI of England. His power base was in Kent. Killed in a skirmish in 1450.

Callisto: Satellite of Jupiter discovered by Galileo.

Lotapes: Mentioned in Pliny's *Natural History* in relation to magic, exorcism, and sorcery. Also a much used feminine name in the Hellenistic world.

Oenone: An abandoned spouse.

Normandy, Nelson, Marathon, Smolensk, My Lai: Sites of massacre and carnage over various points of history without any total resolution.

Marcellus: Roman general in the Second Punic War.

Mark Anthony: Roman general 83 to 30 B.C.; supported Julius Caesar. Defeated by Augustus at the Battle of Actium.

Kutozov: Russian general and diplomat, served 3 Romanov Czars: Catherine, Paul I and Alexander I.

Rommel: German Field Marshall in World War II. Expert in desert warfare. Known as 'The Desert Fox.'

Lysander: General who commanded the Spartan fleet in the Hellespont which defeated the Athenians at Aegospotami in 405 B.C.

Scipio: General who defeated Hannibal at the battle of Zama.

Deinonychus: Agile dinosaurs; grew to about 11 foot long, weighing up to 160 pounds and about 3 to 4 foot in height. Carnivorous. Lived during the early Cretaceous Period about 115 million years ago.

Heinrich Himmler: Chief of German Police in the Reich. Head of the dreaded SS.

SS: "Schutz-Staffel" – Protection squadron formed in April 1925 which had jurisdiction over occupied German Europe. Under Himmler's command the SS were responsible for major crimes against humanity.

Stalingrad: The German war machine broke in the snow "in one of the bloodiest in the history of warfare." Hitler's 6th army was cut off and isolated by cold, hunger, starvation, and relentless Soviet attack. There was incessant house to house fighting out of cubes, thus I use the term "sullen cubistic Stalingrad."

Soso: Creator of mosaics of fishing scenes, of doves drinking from a fountain. The latter painting now held by the Vatican. Originally hailed from Pergamon. His visual motifs scaled to the modern eye emit a literal non-kinetic standardized imagery.

Tauris, Porcius, Aper: Wealthy Pompeians.

Brebix & Nobilior: Prominent gladiators of the period.

Macellum: Marketplace in Pompeii.

Sallust/Golden Cupids/Silver Wedding: These were lodgings of the rich in Pompeii. Now excavated for general viewing. Homes were called a Domus in Latin.

Kaleidoscopic Omniscience

Street of the Tombs, Strada dell'Abbondanza, Caserma dei Gladiatori, Strada Stabiana, Porto Ercolanese: All actual streets or locations in pre-eruption Pompeii.

Fannius Synistor: Well-to-do citizen of Pompeii.

Kobo Abe: "Japanese writer, playwright, photographer, and inventor." Wrote *Woman in the Dunes* which was turned into a film of the same name, directed by Hiroshi Teshigahara.

Archpriest of Hita: "medieval Spanish poet" known for his ribald book *The Book of Good Love*. Original name Juan Ruiz.

Roger Bacon: Astonishing scholar who outraged the thought of "scholastic routine", criticizing the European thought in his great book *Opus Majus*. He was intimately acquainted with the philosophical and scientific insights of the Moorish world, the most advanced civilization at the time. Was imprisoned by the Franciscan order for his views.

Ahmose the 1st: Expelled the Hyksos from Egypt. Under his rule "Egyptian rule reached its peak." Founder of the 18th Dynasty.

Queen Hatshepsut: Fifth pharaoh of the 18th dynasty. Indigenous female ruler who reigned longer than any other female ruler.

Akhenaton: Also ruled as Pharaoh in the 18th dynasty. Known for his focus on "introducing worship centred on Aten as the Sun god". Called in the present era a monotheist.

Biblical 1st Kings: Originally one book with 2nd Kings along with the books of Samuel. The western church separated the Kings and Samuel into two separate books. It is a general condemnation of the "recurrent apostasy of the kings" and their turning away from "God's promise". A book of bitterness, and separation from God's demands.

Coriolanus: Known through Shakespeare for his bravery and courage which lead to eventual assassination. Killed by the Volscians for not attacking Rome.

Syngnathidae: Family of fish which includes sea horses, pipe fishes and weedy and leafy sea dragons.

Sulubika: Great under-recognised flautist in Hawaii.

Gulf of Castellammare: Bay in southern Italy near Naples in the region of Vesuvius.

Eugène Freyssinet: Made a technical leap to "his idea of permanent compression in concrete", practically applying it in 1928. Essential for the modern bridge.

Enver Hoxha: Communist leader of Albania from 1944 until 1985. Anti-revisionist of Marxism-Leninism. Dictator of Albania.

Editor's Postscript

The text layout for the poems follow the author's intentions as well as the aesthetic of the original printed versions from Pantograph Press and Sun & Moon Press. The Endnotes from both those versions have also been duly compiled here. We are pleased to include the author's original pencil drawings from *The Stratospheric Canticles*.

My thanks to Will Alexander, an unparalleled sage and poet from our age, for entrusting these wonderful texts to my care.

www.ingramcontent.com/pod-product-compliance
Lightning Source LLC
Chambersburg PA
CBHW031137160426
43193CB00008B/172